W9-DFL-059

Using the Board in the
Language Classroom

CAMBRIDGE HANDBOOKS FOR LANGUAGE TEACHERS

This is a series of practical guides for teachers of English and other languages. Illustrative examples are usually drawn from the field of English as a foreign or second language, but the ideas and techniques described can equally well be used in the teaching of any language.

In this series:

Drama Techniques in Language Learning – A resource book of communication activities for language teachers *by Alan Maley and Alan Duff*

Games for Language Learning *by Andrew Wright, David Betteridge, and Michael Buckby*

Discussions That Work – Task-centered fluency practice *by Penny Ur*

Once Upon a Time – Using stories in the language classroom *by John Morgan and Mario Rinvolucri*

Teaching Listening Comprehension *by Penny Ur*

Keep Talking – Communicative fluency activities for language teaching *by Friederike Klippel*

Working with Words – A guide to teaching and learning vocabulary *by Ruth Gairns and Stuart Redman*

Learner English – A teacher's guide to interference and other problems *edited by Michael Swan and Bernard Smith*

Testing Spoken Language – A handbook of oral testing techniques *by Nic Underhill*

Literature in the Language Classroom – A resource book of ideas and activities *by Joanne Collie and Stephen Slater*

Dictation – New methods, new possibilities *by Paul Davis and Mario Rinvolucri*

Grammar Practice Activities – A practical guide for teachers *by Penny Ur*

Testing for Language Teachers *by Arthur Hughes*

Pictures for Language Learning *by Andrew Wright*

Five-Minute Activities – A resource book of short activities *by Penny Ur and Andrew Wright*

The Standby Book – Activities for the language classroom *edited by Seth Lindstromberg*

Lessons from Nothing – Activities for language teaching with limited time and resources *by Bruce Marsland*

Beginning to Write – Writing Activities for Elementary and Intermediate Learners *by Arthur Brookes and Peter Gundy*

Ways of Doing – Students Explore Their Everyday and Classroom Processes *by Paul Davis, Barbara Garside, and Mario Rinvolucri*

Using Newspapers in the Classroom *by Paul Sanderson*

Teaching Adult Second Language Learners *by Heather McKay and Abigail Tom*

Teaching English Spelling – A practical guide *by Ruth Shemesh and Sheila Waller*

Using Folktales – *by Eric Taylor*

Personalizing Language Learning – Personalized language learning activities *by Griff Griffiths and Kathryn Keohane*

Teach Business English – A comprehensive introduction to business English *by Sylvie Donna*

Learner Autonomy – A guide to activities which encourage learner responsibility *by Ágota Scharle and Anita Szabó*

The Internet and the Language Classroom – Practical classroom activities and projects *by Gavin Dudeney*

Using the Board in the Language Classroom *by Jeannine Dobbs*

Using the Board
in the Language
Classroom

Jeannine Dobbs

PUBLISHED BY THE PRESS SYNDICATE OF THE UNIVERSITY OF CAMBRIDGE
The Pitt Building, Trumpington Street, Cambridge, United Kingdom

CAMBRIDGE UNIVERSITY PRESS
The Edinburgh Building, Cambridge CB2 2RU, UK
40 West 20th Street, New York, NY 10011-4211, USA
10 Stamford Road, Oakleigh, Melbourne 3166, Australia
Ruiz de Alarcón 13, 28014 Madrid, Spain
Dock House, The Waterfront, Cape Town 8001, South Africa

http://www.cambridge.org

First published 2001

Printed in the United States of America

Typeface Sabon 10½/12 pt.

A catalog record for this book is available from the British Library

Library of Congress Cataloging-in-Publication Data
Dobbs, Jeannine.
Using the board in the language classroom / Jeannine Dobbs.
p. cm. – (Cambridge handbooks for language teachers)
Includes bibliographical references and index.
ISBN 0-521-65417-3 (pbk.)
1. Language and languages – Study and teaching.   2. Blackboards.   3. Teaching – Aids
and devices.   I. Title.   II. Series.
P53.15 .D6 2001
418′.0071 – dc21   00-041459

ISBN 0 521 65417 3   paperback

Contents

Acknowledgments

My thanks go to Penny Ur, for all her help, and to my mentors, teachers, and colleagues from whom, over the years, I have learned so much.

Thanks, too, to my students and dear friends from other countries, for widening my horizons, in particular, José Milton Contreras and his wife, Rosa Téllez; Anh Nguyen and his wife, Sen Thi Vo; Roberto García Pérez and his brother Erlindo; Heike Lewandowski Robinson and her husband, Neil; Brigitt Keller and her husband, Alberto Godenzi; and last but certainly not least, Masako Tsuchida and her husband, Yukihide.

Finally, special thanks to my husband, Otto, for his encouragement and support through this and many other projects.

Memorial marker commemorating Reverend Samuel Read Hall's "pioneer use of the blackboard," erected in 1923 by the town of Concord, Vermont. (*Town of Concord, Vermont, 1781–1976: Then and Now,* compiled by Leah C. Moyse; photograph by Leah C. Moyse)

The inscription reads:

The State of Vermont
erects this tablet August 15, 1923
on the site of the
FIRST NORMAL SCHOOL IN AMERICA
opened March 11, 1823, by its founder
REVEREND SAMUEL READ HALL, LLD
originator of American system
of teacher training
author of first text-book on teaching
published in America
pioneer in the use of the blackboard
as a schoolroom appliance

Introduction

As far as we know, the first teacher who wrote on classroom walls was the Reverend Samuel Reed Hall (1795–1877), an innovative educator and minister who is said to have first written on a piece of dark paper when teaching a mathematics lesson in Rumford, Maine, in 1816. Later Hall moved to Concord, Vermont, where, it is believed, he had the plaster in his classroom painted black. Soon, many other teachers, following Hall's example, painted plaster walls or plain boards black to create a visual teaching aid. By the second quarter of the nineteenth century, enameled walls and then slate boards dominated American classrooms. Hall, who is also credited by American historians with inventing the blackboard eraser and with introducing many other educational innovations, has been honored by the state of Vermont with a memorial in Concord (see photo, p. viii) bearing the inscription including the words "pioneer in the use of the blackboard as a schoolroom appliance" (Levy, p. 39).

In today's classrooms, of course, it is possible to find not only black chalkboards but also green, blue, or other colors, as well as boards of different types of composition such as whiteboards that require dry ink markers instead of chalk. In some classrooms, one also finds flip charts, large tablets of paper used for many of the same purposes and activities as boards. From here on I shall refer to public writing space of these different kinds simply as *the board*.

In spite of the availability of these various kinds of public writing space, however, I have noticed recently that board use in many U.S. schools is declining. In some schools, old boards are being allowed to decay; in many new classrooms, space devoted to boards is decreasing. The reason is not hard to find: Many classrooms now have overhead projectors, movie screens, and TV and computer monitors for student and teacher use. A few even have electronic whiteboards (see Appendix A). Because such equipment not only is expensive to buy and maintain but requires electricity, varying degrees of technological skill, and accessories such as transparencies, film, and software programs, many classrooms – even some in affluent countries – will continue to operate with few or no high-tech tools.

Even when classrooms have access to high-tech tools, however, we should not use these tools at the expense of boards. Boards provide a public writing space that is immediately accessible to both teachers and

1

Remains of a painted plaster wall used as a blackboard in the Fisher School, Westwood, Massachusetts, built in 1845 and restored and preserved by the Westwood Historical Society. (Photograph by Ralph A. Buonopane, courtesy of the Westwood Historical Society.)

students. Teachers can use the board to record messages they especially want their students to remember, to present new information, and to record what students say. Writing on the board is an active, public, physical activity: Students not only can see something happening, they can physically make it happen themselves. Students writing publicly can receive immediate, personal, face-to-face responses from the teacher and from their peers. Teachers can see not only what students are producing (or not producing) but also can read their body language.

Moreover, because different students rely on different learning strategies, they need a variety of learning experiences. When the teacher writes on the board, students whose learning is strengthened by visual stimuli benefit. When students write on the board, students whose learning is strengthened by hands-on, kinesthetic experiences benefit.

When a number of students write on the board simultaneously and the others write at their desks, elements of competition and immediacy are introduced into the classroom chemistry that heighten students' interest.

Students measure themselves against their peers' public writing: Who can write the most, or with the fewest errors, or show (off) the best ideas or finish fastest?

By facilitating our students' use of the board, we increase their share of classroom discourse or "air" time and create multiple opportunities for them to interact with their peers and with us. Finally, writing on the board is active: It gets students on their feet, it adds variety to classroom routines, and best of all, it's fun.

It is time, therefore, that all of us, even teachers who have access to the newest technology, take another look at the humble board. We need to explore teacher use – how the board can be used to help us manage our classrooms and help us teach – and student use – how the board can help our students learn by giving them more opportunities to generate language, more interaction with their classmates and with us, and more responsibility for their own learning process.

Teacher use of the board

The board can help teachers manage the classroom, can be a valuable teaching tool, and can be a way to record student input.

Using the board to help manage classrooms

Classroom experience soon teaches us that when we have an important message to convey to our students, we may need to write the message as well as say it so that our students will have a better chance of understanding and remembering it – and so that they can write it down if they need to. This is especially true of homework assignments, announcements of plans or of items to be brought to class for special purposes, schedules and timetables, and special class rules, if we have them. When students are assigned to groups, confusion may be avoided if we post the names of each group's members as well as each person's duties: Who will lead the discussion, who will record it, who will report it, who will keep track of the time and keep people focused on the task. If students have special classroom roles or duties on a rotating basis such as attendance taker or cleanup, we can record them on the board. Without being intrusive, we can keep students informed of how many minutes remain in timed activities and tests; or we can post scores for competitive activities. It is sometimes effective to display outlines of lesson plans and agendas: If students can see that a fun activity is planned for the end of a class period, they may help us keep to a busy schedule in order to ensure that there will be sufficient time left for it. Or we may want to display information mainly as a reminder to our students and/or to ourselves.

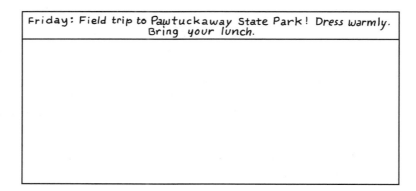

Friday: Field trip to Pawtuckaway State Park! Dress warmly.
Bring your lunch.

Many of these housekeeping messages need to be communicated on a daily basis to keep the class well organized and running efficiently. Writing them on the board can help ensure that our students understand, follow, remember, or record important information; moreover, messages can be used to prevent confusion and to save valuable class time.

Using the board as a teaching tool

In preparation for the day's class, we can use the board as a "get-ready-to-learn" tool. We can write, before or at the beginning of class, provocative quotations or questions, riddles, tongue twisters, scrambled vocabulary words (see Activity A.1.24) or scrambled sentences (see Activity A.3.19). These types of activities give students who arrive early something to get started on, and they help to get everyone focused on English, although, of course, these activities can be used not only as a warm-up but any time during class.

For beginning levels, we might head the board with the day and date. And for all levels, just for fun, we can write greetings and draw illustrations to observe special occasions such as local, national, or religious holidays, birthdays of famous people, and our students' birthdays. Or we can invent occasions like Happy Heat Wave! or Celebrate Spring or Let's Sing Day.

There are many ways the board can be used during class to support teaching. We can, for example, draw stick figures or abstract forms on the board and have students compose oral or written stories about them (see Activities A.4.3 and A.4.6, for example). Or, we can write vocabulary words or questions or statements drawn from a course book

reading or other sources and then ask students to respond orally or in writing in appropriate ways (see Activities A.1.4 and B.3.6). You might want to browse through the index to this book at this point for additional, more specific ideas of board activities you might use to support your own teaching.

Using the board helps students focus on what we are saying when we introduce them to new language concepts, and it helps them understand and remember what they hear. Presenting new material "live" on the board obviously takes longer than giving students a handout with the material already prepared – prepackaged as it were. But in most cases, this additional time is time well invested. As we draw or write on the board, we can explain what our drawing or writing means. When the board is used, students get the information gradually, so that they have the time to question anything they do not understand. If the information is complex, the students have time to grasp small pieces of it as it evolves, rather than looking at a sheet of paper bearing long lists of vocabulary words or complicated instructions or rules. If students then transcribe the information from the board to their notebooks, they make it their own. They write down as little or as much of the information as they feel they need; they process the information as they reproduce it.

In addition to using the board to present new concepts to students, we can use it to explain, clarify, illustrate, emphasize, organize, drill, and list information. We can write key words or a brief outline of our complete presentation. We can give examples of how to use new vocabulary. We can draw stick figures to illustrate grammar points (as in Activity A.3.16) and webs to show relationships between concepts (see Activity A.1.8). We can use the board to amplify and highlight the most important information in our presentations. Students may then elect to copy some or all of this supplemental information into their notebooks. Supplying them with a visual record is extremely important because many students are unable to listen to information delivered in a second language, evaluate what they hear in order to extract the most important information, and then record it.

We can also use board work to determine students' readiness for new material, to review new material, and to assess students' success at mastering this material. Frequent, quick, informal checks of students' achievements, which many of the board activities in this book can provide (e.g., Activities A.1.24, A.3.4, and A.7.1), help to keep us abreast of students' progress, or their lack thereof, easily and without the stress to students that accompanies quizzes and tests, although tests certainly have their place in the curriculum. Furthermore, students may benefit from seeing how well they do in comparison to their peers because it helps them to assess their own achievement levels more realistically.

Finally, we can use the board to quickly summarize the day's important activities, to review a language concept that we have just introduced, or as a lead-in to the next day's class.

TOMORROW:

Jazz
Chants

Using the board to record student input

Just as we use the question-and-answer method to involve our students and enliven and enhance our presentations of new concepts, we can also elicit input from students to make our use of the board more collaborative. We can ask students to brainstorm a topic while we record what they say. We can record questions students ask and the answers that other students offer. We can ask questions and record students' answers.

Michael O'Hare, a supporter of this method of teaching, points out in his article "Talk and Chalk: The Blackboard as an Intellectual Tool" (1993) that the advantage of making a board record is that it can be referred to as long as it remains visible. "What is said out loud," he writes, "must be said to all, but any participant can interrogate the board privately at any time" (p. 241). But, O'Hare warns, teachers should record "participants' contributions in their own words," because if teachers rephrase, students will feel that their comments were somehow "wrong." He also believes that when teachers paraphrase students'

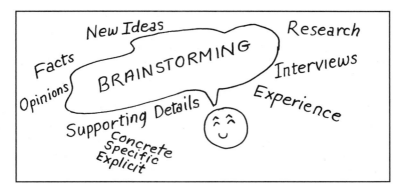

comments, they are exerting a type of control over their students' discourse that tends to "dump them back into 'you talk, we listen' mode" (p. 245). O'Hare, however, is not writing specifically about ESL/EFL students, who make a larger number of erroneous contributions than native speakers do. An exception needs to be made, therefore, to allow for the elimination or correction of erroneous statements. When a student's contribution is not in error but a native speaker might use an idiomatic expression or choose a more precise word, we may want to supplement the student's phrasing with this information in the hope that the student will make it his or her own because it expresses his or her own idea. Of course, one way to avoid the possible problems of paraphrasing, as well as to increase student participation further, is to let students do their own recording.

It is the rare teacher – experienced, new, or in training – who has not used the board as a language teaching tool or been taught by a teacher writing on a board. But many teachers may not be familiar with *students* writing on the board. Thinking back on five years of high school and college-level foreign language classes, I find it difficult to recall ever writing on the board as a student. I now see, however, that my own students look forward to activities that put them at the board and that when they become comfortable using it at my direction, they sometimes initiate using it on their own.

Student use of the board

For students, writing on the board is a hands-on, learning-by-doing activity. What they write publicly usually gets read and responded to immediately. Not only the teacher but also peers become involved in what has been written. It is advantageous, therefore, to have not only individual student scribes use the board but also groups of students working simultaneously while the rest of the students write at their desks. In this way, all members of the class are challenged by the same questions. Students writing at the board often comment spontaneously on each other's content and each other's use of language. Furthermore, students writing at the board often invite their peers' comments because their work is on display and their need to know is great. As they compare their work with that of their peers, their critical faculties are heightened. They learn from their peers' successes and mistakes. Making comparisons, alterations, and corrections helps students become more aware of what revision means. They collaborate and compete. And they become teachers.

Some advantages of having groups of students write publicly at the board are as follows:

- A different atmosphere is created. A group writing at the board is a public group within the whole class, and the students interact not only with those in their group but with the whole class. In contrast, when students collaborate in small groups at their desks, usually little or no interaction takes place between groups.
- No single student can become disengaged and "disappear" without the teacher's notice, as can students in groups at their desks.
- A student cannot monopolize the discourse because written discourse cannot dominate "air time" the way oral discourse can.
- Spontaneous collaboration at the board is a voluntary process in which students can participate or leave at will, unlike the process that occurs when students are grouped at their desks for the specific purpose of editing each other's work or discussing content.
- The teacher's monitoring ability increases. A teacher can "sit in" only on one small group at a time. But, when the board is used, the teacher can observe what is taking place at the board and circulate among students working at their desks, acting as a resource to both groups.

In addition, board work allows us to easily observe students in the act of writing and see how they think in their new language. We see their false starts, their hesitations, and the errors they make but discover for themselves. These observations often lead us to a better understanding of the types of errors they make repeatedly, and of whether or not they doubt the accuracy of their usage. Furthermore, it gives us the opportunity, if we choose, to address difficulties as they arise – to assist by suggesting the word or grammar structure the student seems to be searching for, or to make corrections as problems occur. This immediacy can be very exciting for teachers and rewarding for the students who are intensely aware of their needs at that moment and appreciate having those needs met.

Public writing allows us to emphasize the process rather than the product. By its very nature, board writing is ephemeral and errors are easily erased. Students seem not to become as possessive and sensitive to criticism of their board writing as they do of "finished" writing or of writing that is committed to paper that they can hold in their hands.

Furthermore, some students have more confidence in their written than in their oral discourse and find it easier to participate in written form. Some students dislike asking for help or lack the verbal competence to express their problems and welcome the fact that the teacher or other students can see their problems and offer help when they need it.

Using the board in response to teacher prompts

At the teacher's direction, students can use the board for numerous activities such as practicing and testing their grasp of new forms; paraphrasing or summarizing other writers; generating their own writing; editing their own and their peers' public writing; checking answers to quizzes and tests; playing games; sharing knowledge, personal experiences, and feelings; or sharing information about their countries and their cultures.

In addition, when possible, students can be encouraged to draw illustrations on the board to accompany their writing; research increasingly shows a strong link between drawing and language learning. Mona Brookes, author of *Drawing with Children: A Creative Method for Adult Beginners, Too* (1996), writes, "[Y]ou can learn information eight times faster and retain it eight times longer if you draw what you are learning about" (p. 225).

Spontaneous student use, no teacher input

Students who have been made aware that the board belongs to them as well as to the teacher sometimes write on it spontaneously. They may, unasked, join a group the teacher has appointed to write publicly. Or, they may, for example, decide to write the answers to a quiz on the board, even though the teacher has not announced that this is the method of checking answers that will be used. Still others may use the board to communicate with their classmates or teacher or to show off newly acquired language skills.

My initial enthusiasm for making sure that students view the board as part of their domain was kindled by one beginning learner, an adult who was illiterate in his own language because he had never had the opportunity to go to school and who became so pleased with his growing skills that he began to write "Good Morning!" and other greetings on the board each day as he arrived, making visible his pride and love of learning. This act convinced me of the power of public writing and led me to seek ways of sharing that power with other students as well as with my fellow teachers.

A summary

Writing on the board offers many benefits. When teachers are writing and not just talking, the visual element stimulates students' interest in what they hear. More important, visual materials help students understand and remember the new information teachers are presenting. When students write at the board, their learning experience becomes self-centered and active. And when groups of students write at the board simultaneously, the students feel both challenged by their peers and protective toward them – they share with them and they learn from them.

Looking ahead

The next section of this book, Reminders, Tips, and Suggestions, may help you to use your board more effectively and/or more efficiently.

Then the Activities sections suggest numerous activities that both you and your students can do at the board. If you have an overhead projector or a flip chart, or can easily make handouts or use other kinds of visual aids, many of the activities may be used in these ways. The activities contain sections called *Preparation, Procedure,* and, where appropriate, *Variations,* optional *Follow-up,* and specific *Comments.* Because the appropriate level of many of the activities is apparent or very adaptable, and because you as the teacher know best whether an activity is suitable for your students, I have not defined the activities according to level.

The purpose of the language-based activities in Section A is to present, practice, or test specific lexical, phonetic, or grammatical items (see pages 25–114) as well as to help students attain increased fluency in their writing, reading, listening, and speaking skills (see pages 115–175). In the first three divisions of Section A, you present target forms in vocabulary, pronunciation, or grammar and students then strive to display or use the new information correctly. These activities also offer the opportunity to review material you have already presented or that students have attained by other means such as course book readings. The activities in the next three divisions in Section A aim to improve students' fluency and skill in generating and comprehending written and spoken English. Section A concludes with several activities that provide a way to review or assess students' class work in a specific area or to assess their overall level of comprehension.

The activities in Section B are more open-ended and communicative. They call for the sharing of information that may then be used, for example, to build a sense of community in the classroom, to help set an agenda, or to educate both teachers and students about other countries and cultures while offering students multiple opportunities for language acquisition and analysis (see pages 179–216). The activities in Section B are focused as much on content – what is being said or written – as on how or how accurately it is being said or written. In most of these activities, students express their feelings or opinions or provide information about their lives or cultures. Activities in this section are designed to help students (1) recognize their language-learning needs, (2) become more autonomous learners, and (3) develop increased awareness of both the diversity and the congruence found in the classroom, the community, and the world.

Appendix A looks to the future of public writing surfaces, when more affluent institutions and programs will likely take advantage of technological advances such as electronic whiteboards. In contrast, Appendix B provides instructions for teachers who currently have no board in their classroom but are willing to construct one, as well as information about a product that makes it possible to create a portable, reusable but also disposable whiteboard surface.

Reminders, tips, and suggestions:
Using the board efficiently and effectively

Getting started

1. Start each day with a board that has been washed. Chalkboards can be washed using just warm water and a squeegee; occasionally, add a little window-washing solution to the water. A solution for cleaning whiteboards is available at most stationery stores, or a window-cleaning solution can be used.

   Start each class with a board that has been erased. Vacuum the chalk trays under a chalkboard from time to time to keep the dust that collects there at a minimum.

   Be sure to have sufficient chalk, or felt-tipped markers for whiteboards, as well as sufficient erasers for the number of people who will be writing. Small terry cloth towels are good make-do erasers for whiteboards and can be washed and used indefinitely. To be safe, carry extra chalk or markers and erasers with you in case classroom supplies turn out to be insufficient or missing.

2. As you make your lesson plan, decide whether you will write on the board and when you will do it. Write before the class begins if possible and appropriate. Also decide whether to include board activities for your students. If inspiration strikes or need arises, obviously you would use the board spontaneously as the class proceeds.

3. White chalk shows up well against black or green chalkboards, as does yellow. It is possible to use other colors, but they show up less well on chalkboards. Whiteboard markers come in a multitude of colors that, except for yellow, show up well.

   You may want to have students use a specific color for their writing; this makes it possible for you to do your editing and correcting in another color. Colors also work well to set off designated spaces (areas in which pairs or teams can work simultaneously, for example), or to teach the use of charts and tables, or for emphasis. If you choose to use special colors for specific purposes, try to keep it simple and be consistent.

4. If your students are learning the roman alphabet or just beginning to learn to write in English, you might have permanent lines painted on part of your board space to facilitate this activity. Or you might want permanent lines to keep your own writing on a straight path so that it serves as a model of clarity, neatness, and legibility; slanted writing

can confuse students who are not accustomed to the language or who have learning disabilities.

Layout

1. Feel free to think of your board as any kind of visual space you want it to be. For brainstorming activities and creating webs, you may want to think of it the way an artist thinks of a canvas or the way a movie director thinks of a screen. You may want to begin using the board somewhere in the middle and build out and around some key word(s) or central theme. For other kinds of work, such as writing instructions or assignments, you may want to capitalize on the horizontal nature of the board and define your space as being like the left and right pages of a newspaper or a book. Using this type of layout may particularly benefit students whose first language is not written horizontally, or not from left to right. Draw vertical lines on the board where you want the edges of the "pages" to be.

   Group work at the board, as well as some activities, calls for dividing the board into separate compartments or boxes in which the students write. It helps if you draw these enclosures in a different color from the one the students will use for writing.

2. Most students prefer that teachers print rather than write in script. Except for personal correspondence, most writing in the United States and many other countries is now done with printed letters, so do not be too concerned if you are not exposing your students to English written in script.

   Find out what size letters your students prefer by experimenting. Try using 1-, 1½-, 2-, and 2½-inch (2½-, 4-, 5-, and 6-centimeter) letters; then ask students who sit farthest from the board to tell you which size of lettering they need. As a rule of thumb, I find that printing letters approximately 1½ inches (4 centimeters) high allows students sitting up to 15 feet (4½ meters) from the board to read them comfortably; letters 2 inches (5 centimeters) high can be read at almost twice that distance. With letters of this size, leave 2½ to 3 inches (6 to 7½ centimeters) of space between lines. Check occasionally that your writing can be read by students who sit farthest from it.

3. If you use the board frequently for housekeeping announcements (reminders of work that is coming due or events in the offing, for example), you may want to designate a portion of the board for this purpose. If you are right-handed, you might use the upper-right-hand corner of the board, so that, as you continue to write, your body will not block your students' view, and they can refer to this space at will.

Or, if you are taller than your students, designate a space about 12 inches (30½ centimeters) wide along the entire top edge of the board as "yours." Then always use this space for similar purposes. Students will become accustomed to checking this space for your messages.

Erase out-of-date messages immediately so that students don't lose interest. Write new messages in a different color, perhaps, and draw students' attention to them and/or read them aloud.

4. When recording the answers and comments students make in response to discussion questions, you may wish to write them randomly – thus nonjudgmentally – all over the board as they occur. As the discussion winds down, you may wish to highlight some responses that seem particularly relevant or accurate by underlining or circling them or checking them off. You may even be able to organize and rewrite the rest of the responses in some kind of order – to reflect their merit, for example, or a progression in the thinking that has occurred, or a summary of the discussion.

5. To help focus students on a board activity or task, write a caption, a title, or a question at the top of the board as you begin. Here are a few ideas on how to emphasize these or other special words or phrases:

- Use a different-colored chalk or marking pen.
- Write in LARGER letters.
- Turn a short piece of chalk sideways to create broader letters.
- <u>Underline</u> the words you want to highlight.
- Draw boxes around them.
- Draw "fat" letters like those graffiti artists use.

Illustrations

Sometimes the best way to make instructions come alive or to provide a practice activity for students to do at the board is to draw illustrations. The basic rule for drawing on the board is to keep it simple. You may not be an artist, but you can create almost any illustration you need based on circles, ovals, rectangles, triangles, and straight lines. Here are some principles that have been followed in the line drawings that accompany some of the activities in this book:

People: A standing male figure doing nothing in particular can be indicated by drawing a circle for the head and five lines for the torso, arms, and legs. Add a triangle (skirt), and you have a woman doing nothing in particular.

If the figures are doing something with their arms, bend the elbows. Note that elbows bend at the waistline.

Forget the hands unless the purpose of the illustration is something they are doing with their hands.

If the figures are moving, bend the legs halfway down, at the knees, and add feet. Point the feet in the direction the figure is moving. If the figures are sitting, bend the bodies at the waist.

Faces: To save time, omit features unless their expression is the reason you are drawing the illustration. Practice drawing raised and lowered eyebrows, up- and down-turned or wide-open mouths, until you achieve the mood or feeling you want the face to express.

Animals and objects: Draw rectangles to represent the bodies of most animals when they are walking. Sitting or lying down, their bodies can usually be represented by triangles or circles. Buildings are squares or rectangles; roofs are triangles. Trees are straight lines topped by circles. Vehicles are four-sided figures (trapezoids) or half circles with circles for wheels. You will seldom need to be concerned with perspective. If your drawing needs perspective, just remember that things look smaller the farther they are from the observer. A wide road may narrow to a single, fine line at the "horizon."

For more help with basic illustrations, see Wright and Haleem, *Visuals for the Language Classroom* (1991, pp. 110–116), whose advice forms the basis of much of what I have outlined here. Other helpful texts are Wright, *Pictures for Language Learning* (1990) and Shapiro and Genser, *Chalk Talks* (1994), which contains a dictionary of easy-to-draw symbols.

If you fear drawing even a simple stick figure, or if, on the other hand, you wish to tackle more ambitious drawings but believe that you lack the ability, see Edwards, *Drawing on the Right Side of the Brain* (1993) or *Drawing on the Artist Within* (1986), in which the author shares her method of teaching drawing by having the would-be artist copy a drawing that is upside down. (Try it. It works.) Finally, determine which of your students love to draw and enlist their help.

Ensuring students' success at the board

1. Before you ask students to write on the board, check their access to it. Be sure that the board is easily visible from each student's desk. Also make sure that students can stand at least two deep in front of the board so that pairs can work comfortably when one student is writing and the other is editing or advising. Students will not feel that the board is truly part of their domain if a teacher's large desk blocks them from it, as is the case in many classrooms. Whenever you can, move any obstacle that inhibits students' access to the board(s).

2. When you introduce a board activity to a class, you can do a number of things that will help to ensure that the students will come to appreciate and enjoy the experience. One way to begin is by assigning

written work for all students to do at their desks. Then circulate, looking over shoulders, reading, and perhaps commenting or asking questions. When you have seen enough to determine that a particular student's writing has been fairly well done, tell the writer that you are going to ask a number of students who have written a good response to copy on the board what they have already written and that he or she is one of the selected ones.

Another way to begin is simply to announce that one of your teaching strategies is to have students write at the board, that you usually have a number of students write at the same time, and that you will begin this activity by selecting some good responses to be written there.

What seems to get students off to a good start is knowing that everyone is busy doing something other than staring at them while they write on the board and that they are not going to be working there alone. It also helps if students know that all of their classmates will eventually be writing at the board.

Turn taking can be handled in a number of ways. Here are a few:

- Ask for volunteers to begin, and then call on the rest.
- Have students who have completed their turns at the board select students to replace them.
- Assign turns based on where students are sitting or where their names fall in the alphabet.
- If pairs or groups are already working together because they speak different first languages, use these existing groups for board activities.

Even students with no history of public writing soon learn that writing at the board is not as intimidating as they might fear because public writing is "common property" in a way and is easy to borrow. Often a quick glance at a peer's board space is all that is needed to get students off and running with their own ideas. Thus, public writing done simultaneously has a built-in safety net; and students seldom need suffer the embarrassment or failure that frequently occurs in verbal discussions when students called on are forced to remain silent or to admit, "I don't know."

3. Students writing at the board often benefit from working in pairs. You may want to pair students with differing levels of ability for the purpose of having the more competent student help the other. If you have students with different first languages, consider whether the practice of English is crucial or whether, for the task at hand, it would be more helpful if the partners speak the same first language. In all cases, observe whether the peer tutor is doing too much of the work for the partner. If this happens, allow only one piece of chalk per pair,

and make a rule that the peer tutor's role is to advise verbally rather than to write.

4. Most students enjoy board activities, and these activities have many beneficial features; but like everything else, they can be overdone. Be careful not to kill your students' enjoyment by overusing them.

Correction and evaluation

1. Where correction is concerned, consider the following:

Before your students write at the board, you must decide how much correction of their writing is enough and how much is too much. Ask yourself questions like these: Will all writing on the board be corrected? Who will correct it? How much correction will they do?

My rule of thumb regarding the correctness of work done at the board is this: Although there are times when correction is not the most important issue, in general, work that is presented publicly should be, or at least should end up being, essentially correct. Students frequently copy into their notebooks what appears on the board and sometimes refer to these examples later, using them as models. Therefore, make a special effort to ensure that the final product is correct.

Preselecting good student writing to be displayed on the board (see Ensuring Students' Success at the Board, page 17) is one way to minimize the amount of correction that will need to be done on board work. But the object of some board work is to check for errors and to publicly address the question of how to correct them. If this is the objective, I often proceed in this fashion: First, I ask the writer whether he or she can correct the writing; then I ask the students whether they can do the correcting; finally, if errors remain, I correct the work myself. But very often a student corrects another student's board work. This is one of the advantages of public writing. To encourage students to continue to look critically at a piece of writing after they have "corrected" it, announce that there are still X number of errors and ask whether they can find them. Quite often they can. If they need still more hints, use a colored chalk or marker and circle or underline the mistakes. As a last resort, make the corrections yourself.

But you may not always want to take the time to correct everything. For one thing, writing at the board means that events proceed very quickly. Unlike other kinds of writing activities or assignments, it can move – or can seem to move – at almost the speed of oral communication: A number of students may be writing simultaneously, and students who are working at their desks may require your attention at the same time as those writing at the board.

For another thing, if a board assignment produces numerous kinds of errors, you may want to be selective in the kinds of errors you address so as not to confuse or frustrate students by overcorrecting.

When time is limited or many errors have been made and you are unable to correct everything, decide on priorities. At a minimum, errors involving meaning should be dealt with, as should errors that pertain to the specific board assignment. Thus, if a number of students have gone to the board to write all the idioms using colors that they can think of, you would correct any inaccurate phrases (e.g., "as green as gas" or "paint town red" would be corrected). But if students were writing examples of sentences containing irregular past tense verbs, you would correct errors in those verbs and possibly not correct spelling errors or faulty syntax.

If the board is filled with student writing and you are utterly without time to elicit corrections from students or to make corrections yourself, remember the eraser. A whisk of the eraser through any imperfect writing eliminates it. But if the class is ending and no other class will use the room, consider leaving the offending writing on the board until the class meets again and dealing with it then.

2. Here are some points about evaluation:

A great deal of teacher talk is concerned with making value judgments. We need to encourage our students when their response is correct or their work is good. But these responses can become automatic; if we use them too often, they lose their impact. Listen to how many times per class you say, "Good" or "That's a good guess, but it's not quite right," or something similar. When dealing with public writing, we have options: We can use verbal responses or we can silently reward what is "good" by checking, underlining, circling, or starring it, perhaps with a contrasting color of chalk or marker. Likewise, when something written publicly is incorrect or insufficient, we can silently correct it or call students' attention to it by using chalk or a marker in a color that is different from the color we use to indicate good work, and with our correction marker write a question mark or an X or underline the problem.

Extending the board's usefulness

In *Visuals for the Language Classroom* (1991), Wright and Haleem describe a number of ways to extend the usefulness of the board. They point out that pictures and other realia may be displayed on the surface of a board that has been magnetized. On a whiteboard, in particular, you can use adhesive tape or Blu-tack (a plastic adhesive). You can also display objects by propping them in chalk trays or by running a wire along the top edge of the board and clipping objects to the wire. The area of the board above or below these displayed objects can be used for writing comments. You can also hang a sheet from the wire or clip a large piece of paper to it in order to conceal writing on the board that you do not want students to see until some appropriate time during the class (Wright and Haleem, pages 25–26).

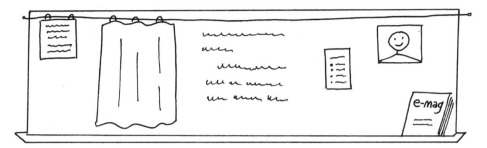

Obviously, it would be possible to mount quite an elaborate production using the board and its extensions. But unless you are convinced that the results are going to be worthwhile, it is better to keep your board productions simple.

Miscellaneous tips

1. Do your board writing before class begins or during a scheduled break if you can. Or, when feasible, have student scribes write on the board for you. They can write key words that you dictate; they can record questions or comments made by their peers. Of course, student scribes write more slowly than you do and may not write as clearly or as accurately. On the other hand, you don't need the writing practice, and they do.

2. Except when students are acting as scribes for the class or when who wrote what is not important, students writing on the board, individually or in pairs, should sign their names or, to save space, their initials to their work. You have enough to attend to in a typical classroom without having to try to remember, after they sit down, which student was responsible for which piece of writing. Get them in the habit of signing their work from the beginning, and life will be simpler.

3. Writing on a chalkboard is not without problems. Chalk creates dust, it wears away quickly, and when mishandled, it – as well as fingernails – can produce some almost unbearable sounds. To help avoid unwanted chalk noise, use soft chalk; and once the end of a new piece

of chalk has taken on a rounded shape, break the chalk and write with the sharp edge.

4. The whiteboard does not lack for drawbacks either. Be sure to use dry-erase markers made especially for whiteboards and not regular, permanent markers, or you will have to clean the board with a solvent. Be aware, as well, that even dry-erase markers can be difficult to erase, that they stain fingers and clothes, and that they have an annoying habit of getting lost. Uncapped markers dry up quickly, so check that caps are securely on the pens. Store markers in a vertical position with their tips pointed down, or they will seem to have dried up when you next try to use them.

5. No matter how attentive your students are, you will not want to turn your back to them for long periods of time. Stand with your body at a right angle to the board as much as possible. (It's something like keeping a car on the road while looking out the side window.) If you are speaking to your class while you are writing or drawing, you will naturally increase the volume of your voice; but if your writing takes more than a minute or two, you might want to alternate writing and speaking.

    If you need to concentrate on what you are doing at the board, assign students an activity to do at their desks so that they have something more to do than simply watch. If the activity can be done with a partner, so much the better. Talking with a peer will probably involve them more than watching the teacher.

6. When you complete a board activity and start a new one, erase the *entire* board, not just enough for your immediate needs. Board leftovers can be very confusing to students.

7. Finally, if other teachers use your classroom after you leave, professional courtesy dictates that you erase your board at the end of your class.

A Language-based activities

A.1 Vocabulary

Writing a new word on the board as we pronounce it, providing stimuli both visually and audibly at the same time we display correct spelling, is only the beginning of how we can use the board to help students learn new words. We can also use the board to:

- Illustrate how to break some words into analyzable parts.
- Write a definition or definitions of a word and provide examples of its use in various contexts.
- Draw a representation of a word or provide opportunities and means for students to imagine or draw a representation of a word.
- Display activities, games, and exercises for students to do using a new word – including those that link it to their previous knowledge and those that require that they generate the new word.

Some of the activities in this section call for students to write original sentences illustrating that they know the meaning of a word. I recommend that you ask students to write sentences that are true to their own experiences or to their own knowledge, because these sentences are more meaningful to the writer and more interesting (more authentic) to the readers.

The sentences should also demonstrate that the writer knows the meaning of a word, and hasn't just inserted it in a sentence correctly. For example, "I told my mother a white lie yesterday" is grammatically correct, but the sentence doesn't show that the writer knows what a white lie is. "I told my mother a white lie yesterday because I didn't want to hurt her feelings" both uses the idiom correctly and shows that the writer knows its meaning.

Because repetition seems to be the most important factor in long-term retention of new vocabulary, students must have multiple, varied opportunities, at levels appropriate to their competencies, to experience (both to receive and to generate) each new word. I urge, therefore, that when you work with students to increase their vocabulary, you select not just one of the activities that follows but three or four over a period of several classes and, at the same time, that you encourage students to maintain their own, customary ways of reviewing and memorizing new words outside the classroom.

Language-based activities

A.1.1   Charting new words
A.1.2   Constructing sentences using new vocabulary
A.1.3   Visual imaging
A.1.4   Categorizing vocabulary
A.1.5   Reviewing thematic vocabulary
A.1.6   Word forms
A.1.7   Co-occurrence
A.1.8   Association webs
A.1.9   Word study webs
A.1.10 Etymology
A.1.11 Ranking words
A.1.12 What's the weather?
A.1.13 Naming: Colors, parts of the body, and clothing
A.1.14 Parts of the body
A.1.15 Let's go food shopping
A.1.16 Putting things away
A.1.17 Telling time in English
A.1.18 Name that (cardinal) number
A.1.19 Ordinals and dates
A.1.20 What's my line?
A.1.21 Idioms
A.1.22 Do or make?
A.1.23 Homonyms
A.1.24 Reviewing and assessing new vocabulary
A.1.25 More reviewing and assessing of new vocabulary
A.1.26 Vocabulary stepping-stones
A.1.27 Do you remember?
A.1.28 Vocabulary ticktacktoe
A.1.29 Blankety-blank
A.1.30 Make a new word
A.1.31 Playing with words

See also:

A.2.4   Does it rhyme? (pronouncing and reviewing new vocabulary)
A.2.9   Multiple-syllable homographs (look-alike words that differ in pronunciation)
A.4.3   She says/he says (dialogue based on new vocabulary)
A.5.1   From A to Z (names of letters)
A.5.6   Abbreviations: Common and academic
A.6.1   Write the numbers (names of numbers)
A.6.3   Writing, illustrating, and performing dialogues and skits (dialogue based on new vocabulary)
A.6.7   Hamburger dictation (food)
A.6.8   Constructing a jigsaw picture (geometric forms)

A.1.1 Charting new words

Recording new words as they emerge in the classroom context.

Procedure: Keep your colored chalk or markers handy, and as the class encounters a new word, write it on the board using a different color for different word forms (e.g., black for nouns if you have a whiteboard or white on a chalkboard, red for verbs). As you write the new word, give a short oral definition of it.

At the beginning of the next class, quickly review the list. Then add new words that come up in this class and other words until you feel that there are enough words for a general overall review and a quiz if you desire one.

Follow-up: Once you believe that the new words are becoming part of the students' vocabulary, you may wish to help them to determine any affixes that can be used with the new words. Write affixes, also in a different color, alongside the base word. Do the same with antonyms and synonyms.

Acknowledgment: I learned this activity from Ray Clark at a Northern New England TESOL conference (1994).

A.1.2 Constructing sentences using new vocabulary

Preparation: Choose five to fifteen words that were introduced and discussed during a previous class.

Procedure: For each word you have chosen, give students a definition and ask for the word. When you hear the correct word, ask for its spelling. When you hear the correct spelling, write the word on the board.

If the word has important secondary definitions, ask students whether they know them. If they don't know them, write the other definitions on the board.

Then ask students to write original sentences that illustrate the major meaning(s) of the word. Be sure that the sentences are true to the students' own experiences or knowledge and that they illustrate that the students know the meaning of the word, not merely how to insert the word into a sentence.

Choose students to write their sentences on the board.

Variation: Scatter ten to fifteen words randomly across the board. Ask students to create sentences using two or more of the new words.

Call on students to recite their sentences; as they do, link the new words using colored chalk.

Leave the linked words on the board; and later in the class, challenge students to repeat the sentences represented by the colored lines.

Comment: Constructing sentences is a good activity for practicing words students need in their active (i.e., speaking or writing) vocabulary.

A.1.3   Visual imaging

Presenting the key word (mnemonic) method of vocabulary building.

Procedure: On the board write a word your students need in their vocabulary. Next to it, if you are an EFL teacher and speak your students' first language, write a word in that language that sounds like the new word. For example, suppose that you are teaching English to Spanish speakers, and the English word you are teaching is *parrot.* You might write the Spanish word *perro* ("dog") next to it since these two words sound and even look fairly similar.

If your students are multilingual, explain that they should choose a word in their native language that sounds like the target word to use as their mnemonic device.

The next step is to invite students to visualize the new word and the sound-alike key word in a relationship with each other. Thus, they might picture the dog with a parrot riding on its back.

Finally, invite students to try out the process on their own. Give them a new target word, and ask them to think of a sound-alike word in their first language, so that they can visualize the relationship and (optional) produce a drawing that will help them remember the new word.

Comment: If time allows, having students draw the image is fun and can promote retention.

A.1.4 Categorizing vocabulary

Procedure: Draw a grid on the board like the one shown here. Choose a subject area whose vocabulary you want to develop with your students, and elicit all the words they already know connected with it. Then add any other words connected with the subject that you want to teach.

Ask students to help you place all the words in the proper categories of the grid. Illustrate the words if you wish.

Example:

Produce

	Fruit	Vegetables
strawberry		
onion 		
potato 		
cherry		
pineapple 		
pear		

After the words have been successfully placed on the grid, erase them, leaving the grid. See how much your students can reconstruct from memory. Have several volunteers do this activity "live" at the board while the others do it at their desks.

Additional examples:

Animals

	Wild	Domestic
wolf		
dog		
elephant		
horse		
goose		
fox		

Emotions

	Pleasant	Unpleasant
fear		
joy		
worry		
love		
grief		

Language-based activities

Jobs

	Indoor	Outdoor
landscaper		
tailor		
roofer		
secretary		

Positive and negative adjectives

	Positive	Negative
beautiful		
ugly		
honest		
cheerful		
boring		
legal		
second-rate		

Transitive and intransitive verbs

	Transitive	Intransitive
lie		
throw		
sit		
rise		
go		
set		
lay		
raise		

Follow-up: At your next class, you may want students to re-create a grid on the board for review.

A.1.5   Reviewing thematic vocabulary

Procedure: Choose a topic you have been using that has provided a number of new vocabulary words.

Write the word for the general topic area at the top of the board; then make a list of the letters of the alphabet. Group X, Y, and Z together. If you have a large class or want to encourage a number of students to participate at the same time, spread the letters of the alphabet over a wide area of your board space.

Ask students to write a word associated with the topic next to each letter of the alphabet. You may call on individual students or allow students to participate voluntarily.

Words should relate in some way to the topic. More than one word per letter of the alphabet may be given; but some letters may have to be left vacant, depending on the topic. Give hints if necessary.

Example 1:

Fruit

A = apple
B = banana, bunch, blueberry
C = citrus, coconut, crop
D = delicious
E = edible
F = fresh
G = grapes, grapefruit, green, grove
H = healthy
I = insecticide, irrigate
J = juice, juicy
K = kiwi, kumquat
L = lime, lemon, lemonade

M = melon, mango, mulberry
N = nutritious
O = orange, orchard
P = peach, pit, peel, pulp, pear
Q = quince
R = red, rhubarb, rind, raspberry
S = strawberry, stem, seed, skin
T = tasty, tree
U = useful
V = vitamins, vineyard
W = watermelon
X, Y, Z = yellow

Example 2:

Parts of the body

A = Adam's apple, ankle, appendix, artery
B = bones, bowels, blood
C = chin, cheek
D = dimple
E = ear, eye, elbow, eyebrow, eyelash
F = foot, finger, forehead
G = groin, gums
H = head, hair, heart, heel, hip
I = iris, intestines, instep
J = joint
K = knee, kidney
L = lip, lung, liver

M = muscle, mouth, mole
N = nose, neck, nails, nostril
O = organs
P = pancreas, pupil, palm
Q =
R = rib
S = skin, shoulder, shin, stomach
T = tongue, tooth, toe, thumb, throat, thigh
U =
V = veins
W = wrist, wart
X, Y, Z =

A.1.6 Word forms

Procedure: Draw a table on the board consisting of four columns headed *noun, verb, adjective,* and *adverb.* Using a list of vocabulary words that students are working with, fill in each word under its proper heading.
Example 1:

Noun	Verb	Adjective	Adverb
	care		
		explosive	
revelation			

Next, challenge students to fill in as many of the empty spaces for each word as they can. (I allow students to use dictionaries after they have supplied the words they already know.) You may write the answers the students supply, or a scribe may do the writing, or you may assign individual students to one or more words.
Example 2:

Noun	Verb	Adjective	Adverb
care	care	careful	carefully
explosion	explode	explosive	explosively
revelation	reveal	—	—

Comment: For additional word form lists, see Richard Yorkey, *Checklists for Vocabulary Study* (1981).

A.1.7 Co-occurrence

Associating related words.

Procedure:

1. Draw a table on the board containing three columns, headed *Verbs,* *Adjectives,* and *Other.* Above the table write a specific noun that students have recently encountered in their course book or other source and that they need to move to their long-term memories.
2. Have students brainstorm verbs, adjectives, and other nouns that they already know and that they associate with the specific noun, and enter these words in the appropriate columns. Add other words that you feel the students should know.

Example:

College

Verbs	Adjectives	Other
attend	2-year	course
teach in or at	4-year	degree
graduate from	technical	midterm exam
go to	junior	final exam
	freshman, etc.	spring break

3. Finally, discuss the meanings of the words that were new to the students.

Follow-ups:

1. Have students pick words from the table that were new to them and use them in a written or oral sentence. Choose some students to display their sentences on the board.
2. Challenge students to find out who can write a grammatical sentence using the largest number of words on the list.

Variation: If students are working with new verbs, head the columns *Nouns, Adjectives,* and *Other.* If they are working with new adjectives, head the columns *Nouns, Verbs,* and *Other.*

A.1.8 Association webs

New words and words that may be used in the same context with these new words.

Procedure: In the center of a large expanse of board, write a word that students are learning or one that is a key word in content they are studying. Draw a circle around the word.

Ask students to tell you words that they associate with the central word. Write these words around the central word, circle each one, and link it to the central word by a straight line:

Words we associate with *weather*

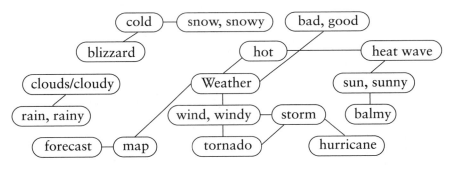

Using different-colored chalk or markers to circle or underline the different parts of speech can be effective.

Variations:

1. If the central word is a noun, ask students to give you adjectives that go with it, verbs it could act upon, or verbs that could act upon it.
2. If the central word is a verb, ask students to give you adverbs that go with it, nouns that could be its subjects, and nouns that could be its objects (if the verb is transitive).
3. Ask students to give you words that begin with the same letter or with the same sound as the central word.
4. Ask students to give you words of the same "class" (e.g., sad words, words that have a homonym, pronouns, words spelled with *i* after *e*).
5. Give students a superordinate as the central word and ask them to give you subordinates (e.g., *animal:* horse, cat, elephant).

37

A.1.9 Word study webs

New words and their functions, connotations, derivations, affixes, synonyms or antonyms, collocations, and/or etymology as well as their definitions (a more advanced version of the preceding activity).

Procedure: Begin by writing the target word in the center of the board. Depending on the word and the level of your students, write headings such as *Definitions, Parts of speech, Connotations, Derivations, Affixes, Synonyms, Antonyms, Collocations,* and *Etymology* around the target word. Draw large circles around these headings and connect them to the central word with straight lines.

Ask students to brainstorm to determine what they already know about the word, and ask them to record their contributions in the appropriate circles. Ask students to use their dictionaries to supply additional information and record it.

Finally, record any further information that you can contribute.

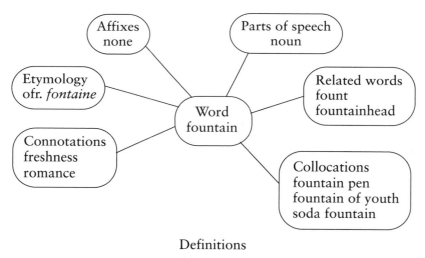

Definitions

1. a spring
2. a point of origin, a source
3. a device that produces a stream of water

Follow-ups:

1. Have students write sentences using the target word with a definition that they did not know before or using a form of the word that they did not know before. Be sure that their sentences illustrate that they know the meaning of the word, not merely how to insert it in a sentence.

2. Using other new words or allowing students to select their own, assign word study webs as homework.

   If all students have worked on the same words, have them put their webs on the board so that they can compare them with those of their peers. Or have them compare their homework in small groups or with a partner.

   If students have worked with different words, have them put their results on the board to share with their classmates.

Comment: When you present different target words, always draw the headings in the same place. This helps students use their visual memory of the webs when trying to recall information about the target words.

A.1.10 Etymology

Listing words according to their roots in order to introduce new words and to facilitate retention.

Procedure: Write a common word root and its meaning(s) on the board.

   Have students volunteer words they already know whose meanings reflect the meaning of the root.

   Then add to the list other words and their meanings that you judge are important for your students to know.

Example:

port (to carry)
deport
export
import
portable
report
portfolio
porter

   Provide immediate practice with the words by having students compose sentences using them either orally or in writing done directly on the board or at their desks. If they write at their desks, choose some sentences to be displayed on the board.

Follow-up: Either later in the same class or during a subsequent class, display only the roots and the new words on the board, and ask for definitions.

Comment: Recalling what words have in common makes it easier to remember or reconstruct what they mean. There is a caveat, however: Although knowing the meaning of some common roots can help sometimes to figure out the meaning of unknown words, it can also lead to faulty reasoning. For example, the root *cumb* means "lie

Language-based activities

down." This helps us understand *recumbent* or *succumb* but not *encumber* or *cumbersome*. Therefore, although students can use etymology to help them make educated guesses about the meaning of unknown words, when doing so, they should also carefully consider context.

Other roots that might be helpful to students are the following:

cap/capit (head): capital, captain, caption, decapitate
card/cord/cour (heart): cardiac, courage, encourage, cordial
cred (to believe, trust): credible, credentials, creed
dic/dict/dit (to say, tell, use words): dictate, dictionary, diction, ditto, edict, verdict
flu/flux (to flow): fluid, fluent, fluctuate, influx
gen (birth, creation, race, kind): generate, generous, gender, genial, progeny
loc/log/loqu (word, speech): colloquial, dialogue, eloquent
mal/male (bad, ill, evil, wrong): dismal, malady, malevolent, malicious
nov/neo (new): innovate, neonatal, neophyte, novel, novelty, renovate
pac/peac (peace): appease, pacify, peace
plex/plic/ply (to fold, twist, tangle, bend): complex, complicate, duplicity, ply
scribe/scrip (to write): inscribe, inscription, manuscript, scribe, script
tain/ten/tin (to hold): contain, retain, pertinent, tenacious
us/ut (to use): abuse, usable, usage, utensil, utility
vers/vert (to turn): avert, convert, divert, diverse, revert, subvert, versatile, vertigo
voc (to call): convocation, evocative, vocabulary, vocation

Variations: Follow the same procedure to introduce prefixes and suffixes:

Prefixes:
il-, im-, dis-, non- (not, negative)
il-: illegal, illiterate, illogical
im-: immobile, immoral, immune, impede, impossible, impolite
dis-: disagree, discontented, discontinue, disfavor, disgrace, displace
non-: nonsense, noncredit, nonentity
re- (again, back): rearrange, recall, repay, replace, rewrite
trans- (across, beyond, change): transfer, transform, transport, transient, transmit
para- (next to, near, beside, beyond): parallel, paramedic, paranormal

Suffixes:
-able, -ible (capable, susceptible, worthy of): bearable, credible, doable
-ful (full of): cheerful, harmful, successful, thankful, useful
-ist (one who performs, works at, specializes in, is characterized by a particular trait or quality): artist, biologist, communist, pacifist

-ment (action, process): attainment, involvement, reinforcement
-scape (view, scene): cityscape, landscape, seascape
-ward (in a specific direction): backward, upward, westward

Comment: More roots and their offshoots can be found in Adam
  Robinson and the Staff of *The Princeton Review, Word Smart:
  Building an Educated Vocabulary* (1994).

A.1.11 Ranking words

Ordering words according to shades of meaning.

Procedure: Help students see the different qualities of words with similar
  lexical meanings by having them place the words on a ladder. For
  example, have them order words placing those with greatest intensity
  at the top:

furious

angry

mad

displeased

  Demonstrate how this works with one or two examples on the
board; then have pairs of students work at their desks with other sets
of words given in random order, such as *cherish, idolize, love, adore,
worship,* and *fancy; disagreeable, nasty, mean, grumpy, crabby,
moody, surly,* and *out of sorts; fall, decline, decrease, drop,* and *crash.*
  Choose students who have different solutions to display their
ladders on the board for discussion.

Variation: Instead of ladders, have students place words on a grid:

Attitudes toward work:

drone	goldbrick	lazy	idler
lazy	slave	diligent	loafer
workaholic	drudge	slacker	eager beaver
industrious	slothful	hard-working	hustler

	Works hard	Hardly works
positive		
negative		

A.1.12 What's the weather?

Procedure: Draw illustrations on the board that portray different kinds of weather.

Examples: Under each illustration write the word or phrase that describes the weather being depicted: *cloudy, partly sunny, sunny, rainy, windy, calm, stormy, snowy.*

Next, point at each illustration and pronounce the accompanying word. Then have the class as a whole repeat the word and have individual students repeat it. Go through each word in turn.

When the students have had enough practice with the new terms, erase the terms. Point to each illustration in turn and ask, "What's the weather?"

Repeat these steps for each illustration in turn; then erase the illustrations.

Follow-ups:

1. Review by redrawing the illustrations in a different order and without the prompts.
2. As homework, immigrant or international students can find the weather forecast for their home country by watching a national weather report on TV or by consulting the Internet and can report their findings to the class.

Variations: Follow the same procedure using illustrations that portray other subjects such as facial expressions, animals, clothing, colors, body parts, household objects, and food.

A.1.13 Naming: Colors, parts of the body, and clothing

Procedure: Have students draw and color representations of themselves on paper. Use 8½ × 11 inch (A4) or larger paper depending on the size of your class and how far from the board students are sitting. Or, if you have a small class, see the Variation below.

If your students drew their "paper doll" on paper, have them cut it out, and attach each cutout to the board with tape or a plastic adhesive such as Blu-tack, allowing space for writing around each one. If you don't even have enough board space to display each student's small cutout figure, use a third of the cutouts for the first part of this activity (names of colors), another third for the second part (body parts), and the remaining third for the final part (clothing).

Assuming that the students are already somewhat experienced with the roman alphabet, write on the board the name of one of the colors present in one or more of the figures.

Pronounce the word and point to the figures in which the color is present.

Have students whose figures contain the color go to the board and copy the name of the color on the board next to the place where the color appears. Then repeat the steps with other colors.

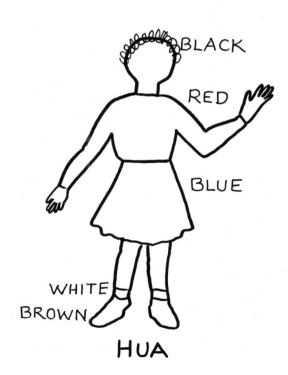

Erase the board writing.

At the next class have students go to the board and label as many of the colors they can remember. Repeat the reviewing process until the students have mastered the colors.

If it is necessary to free the board for other uses until you need the cutouts again, they can be easily taken down and stored.

Variation for small classes: If you have enough board space to display life-size cutouts of all of your students, especially if they are young learners, divide your class into pairs and have them take turns lying on a piece of butcher paper or newsprint large enough to fit their body. Have each partner sketch the outline of his or her partner's body.

Young learners enjoy the novelty of this approach, and the interaction between the pairs as they draw each other is an added benefit and a good icebreaker if used at the beginning of a term. In addition, students sometimes assume humorous poses that can increase the possibilities for vocabulary building such as *dancing, kicking,* or *waving.*

Follow-ups: Use the same procedure to teach parts of the body and/or clothing.

Acknowledgment: I learned this activity from my friend Marilyn Zuckerman.

A.1.14 Parts of the body

Procedure: Explain to the students that they are going to create their own monster or animal or alien. Ask a student who particularly likes to draw to do the necessary drawing on the board, or do it yourself.

To begin, ask the class to vote by voice or by a show of hands for the type of features they want drawn. Ask, for example, "Does the monster have a big head or a little head?" "Hair or no hair?" "Curly hair or straight hair?" Then, encourage students to volunteer information for the drawing without your prompting.

Label the body parts and the features.

When the drawing is complete, review the new vocabulary; then erase the labels and ask students, for example, "What kind of hair does the monster have?"

Optional follow-up: You can continue the activity and provide practice for your students in asking their own questions by having them create a life for the monster.

Have them pick a category such as what the monster eats, where it lives, or what it does. One student imagines a food, for example. The others ask, "Is it sweet?" "Is it green?"

Drawing and labeling can also be done for this part of the activity.

Acknowledgment: This activity is based on one by Chris Murphy, "Dave's ESL Cafe: ESL Ideas from 1996." <www.eslcafe.com> (June 15, 1998).

A.1.15 Let's go food shopping

Preparation: If your students are not already familiar with the names of foods, you may want to take your class to a local food store or market and/or bring to class items from your own kitchen or pictures of foodstuffs in order to prepare students for this activity.

Procedure: On the board draw six containers: a bag (or sack), a can, a box, a bottle, a carton, and a jar. If you have sufficient board space, make each container large enough for students to write the names of up to twenty items in it.

Then divide your class into two teams, assigning each team a different color of chalk or marker. The teams take turns, and students in each team take turns.

Next, from a list of common foodstuffs such as the one on the next page read one item at a time. Have one student from the first team write the name of the item in (or under) the illustration(s) of the container(s) in which the item is prepackaged or is placed at the time of purchase. To save time, have the other team's writer go to the board while the student from the first team is writing.

juice	cereal	coffee
peas	muffins	bread crumbs
celery	ice	soap
ice cream	jam	nuts
beans	bread	lettuce
crackers	cookies	bananas
soup	salt	butter
flour	ketchup	olive oil
soda	potato chips	corn meal
donuts	milk	buns
mustard	salad dressing	

Teammates can prompt, and they can help with spelling.

The other team can challenge if the team members believe that an item has been inappropriately categorized, but it will soon become obvious to all that many items can correctly be placed in more than one category (e.g., *cookies* can go under *box* or *bag*).

Note that you can call out the names of items in any order you want, so you can keep the "score" quite even and perhaps even arrange a tie, if you want to.

Follow-up: Write the following names of measurements on the board, leaving room under each one for students to write the names of foodstuffs.

pound (kilo)	ounce (gram)	loaf
dozen	head	bunch
box	jar	bag
quart (liter)	each	bottle
gallon (liter)	can	bar

Point out that some packaging (name of a container) may also be used for measurement purposes, for example, box, jar, bottle.

Proceed as above, having students write the names of the foodstuffs as they are read under the measurement(s) commonly used to sell them (e.g., *bananas* can go under *pound, dozen, bunch,* and possibly even *each*).

Follow-up: You might want to use Activity A.1.16, Putting things away, in conjunction with this activity.

A.1.16 Putting things away

Reviewing names for clothing, household items, food, and such.

Procedure: On the board sketch a chest of drawers and a clothes closet
(door open). Draw them large enough so that students can write the
names of clothing items on them.

Send two students to the board, one to enter words on the drawing
of the chest, the other to enter words on the closet. Students at their
seats may take turns calling out the names of common items of
clothing. The students at the board must decide whether the item goes
in "their" space.

Students will soon see that some items may be correctly claimed by
both board writers. If a board writer claims an item in error, however,
such as shoes in the drawer, or fails to claim an item, or claims an item
and misspells it, that writer loses his or her turn. The student whose
item ousted the board writer may now do the board writing unless that
person has already had a turn, in which case the board writer can
choose the replacement.

Variations:

1. To practice vocabulary for items commonly found in the kitchen,
   draw a large sketch representing a cupboard above a sink, with
   another cupboard on one side of the sink and a series of drawers on
   the other; next to these, draw a two-door refrigerator:

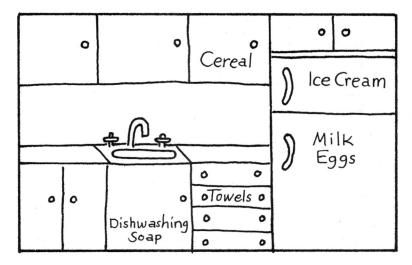

Proceed as above: Ask students to call out the names of common fresh, canned, and frozen food; cleaning supplies such as dishwashing soap; dishes; pots and pans; silverware; table linens. For this variation more than two students can do the board writing.

You might want to use Activity A.1.15, Let's go food shopping, in conjunction with this variation.

2. Work with vocabulary related to other locations, for example, items found on shelves versus those found on a desk or items found in an attic versus those found in a garage, and illustrate appropriately.

A.1.17 Telling time in English

Procedure: Review the numbers 1 through 59 with your students.

Then write on the board and review the words that we commonly use to describe time when we are being exact, for example, *after, before, to* (or *till*), *exactly, a quarter,* or *half past.*

Next, draw a digital clock face on the board and have the students read the time to you using the vocabulary you have practiced. Erase the time and repeat the process using new numbers. Do the same using a clock face with hands, drawing and erasing the hands.

Finally, write on the board and review the words that we commonly use when we speak of approximate time, for example, *about, almost, around*. Draw a clock face with hands and illustrate times that can be used with these approximations.

Follow-up: Divide your class into teams; each team needs enough board space for its work. Have one member from each team go to the board and draw a large clock face with hands.

Team members should take turns calling out a time for the board writer to draw on the clock. If the writer makes an error, or after five correct responses have been given, the writer chooses a teammate to take over the board work.

A.1.18 Name that (cardinal) number

Procedure: Write numbers, scattered randomly, across the board. Call on students or ask for volunteers to tell you the name for each number.

Follow-up: Divide the numbers on the board into three groups (separated by lines) and divide your class into three groups. Have each group send a scribe to the board.

Example:

24 20 11	9 29 5	14 25 five
4	90	1,000 1 twenty-five 15
70 21	2 17	23 30
16	22 19	10 ten
sixteen		
12 7	60 13	6 27
twelve 40 28	sixty	
	26 1,000,000	80
8 100	one million 3	18 50

The "winner" is the group that can correctly spell, and its scribe write, the correct name under each number in his or her allotted space before the other groups have finished. Teammates can help the scribe verbally, but cannot write.

A.1.19   Ordinals and dates

Procedure: On the board, draw a page of a calendar showing the current or forthcoming month. Under the calendar, write the endings for ordinal numbers and, under them, list sufficient cardinal numbers and their ordinal equivalents to make it possible for you to explain how ordinals work:

Example:

MONTH

S	M	T	W	T	F	S
	1	2	3	4	5	6
7	8	9	10	11	12	13
14	15	16	17	18	19	20
21	22	23	24	25	26	27
28	29	30	31			

-st
(1) first
(21) twenty-first

-nd
(2) second
(22) twenty-second

-rd
(3) third
(23) twenty-third

-th
(4) fourth
(19) nineteenth
(24) twenty-fourth
(29) twenty-ninth

-ieth
(20) twentieth
(30) thirtieth

Begin by pronouncing each number, emphasizing the ordinal ending. Then have students practice pronouncing the numbers as a group and individually.

Once students have had sufficient time to practice pronouncing the numbers, do some or all of the following activities:

51

Language-based activities

1. Randomly point to dates on the calendar and have students pronounce and/or spell the ordinal numbers.
2. Randomly point to dates on the calendar and have students write the ordinal equivalents.
3. Ask students questions such as:

   - The first Tuesday of this month is the second. What date is the third Tuesday?
   - If a person gets paid on the last day of the month, when does that person get paid this month?
   - The doctor wants to see me next Friday. What is the date that day?
   - On what dates does our class meet next week?
   - On what date is the third Saturday this month?
   - On what date is the first Monday after the second Sunday?
   - If you have a birthday this month, what is the date and what day does it fall on?

4. Ask the questions in item 3, and have students write the answers, using the ordinal abbreviations: twenty-first, thirtieth, and so on.

Follow-up: To review during a subsequent class or classes, draw only the calendar on the board and repeat the activities.

Comment: If you have a multicultural class, determine whether any of your students' cultures begin their weeks and their calendars with a day other than Sunday; these students may need extra help working with a "Sunday" calendar.

A.1.20   What's my line?

Associating vocabulary with various occupations.

Preparation: Compose a list of four verbs that describe activities associated with a specific occupation. Below the list of verbs, list two or more nouns that are clues to the verb list. Try to make the clues increasingly obvious.

Example:

questions	(v.)
listens	(v.)
examines	(v.)
explains	(v.)
white coat	(n.)
stethoscope	(n.)

(Answer: doctor)

Procedure: Tell students that (1) you have composed a list of words that are clues to people's professions, (2) you are going to copy your list item by item onto the board, and (3) as soon as they think that they know what the occupation is, they should call it out. Write slowly to give students a chance to think and to make guesses.

Follow-up: When you have done this basic activity as a model, have students write their own lists of verbs and nouns, independently, without sharing them with their peers.

The student who has correctly guessed the occupation from your model gets to repeat the procedure, writing his or her list on the board. If a student who has already written is the winner again, that student should call on a peer who has not yet written publicly until all students have had a chance to do so.

Variation for large classes: Divide students into pairs or teams; then have them collaborate on writing lists and choose who is to be the board writer.

Additional examples:

walks	sits or stands	loosens
talks	talks	tightens
writes	questions	greases
serves	grades	tunes up
tables	books	wires
menus	papers	valves
food	homework	engines
(Answer: server)	(Answer: teacher)	(Answer: mechanic)

memorizes	climbs
practices	prunes
performs	sprays
records	picks
notes	trees
scales	fruit
music	apples
(Answer: singer)	(Answer: orchard worker)

A.1.21 Idioms

Procedure: Choose idioms that can be easily visualized and that have a strong link between their literal and their figurative meanings, such as idioms that make comparisons or contain colors or numbers.

Illustrate each idiom on the board, label it, and then explain it:

AS LIGHT AS A FEATHER:

This example needs little if any explanation if students understand the word *feather*. In this case, then, you can give an example of a sentence using the idiom, such as "I took so few clothes with me on vacation that my suitcase was as light as a feather," and ask students to explain it, or you can ask them to compose a sentence using the idiom that shows that they know its meaning.

AS QUICK AS A WINK:

An eye blinks rapidly: therefore, this idiom means to "take very little time." Usage: A race car driver must respond to danger as quick as a wink.

ONCE IN A BLUE MOON:

Literally, a *blue moon* is the second full moon to occur in one calendar month; on average, a blue moon occurs once every 2 1/2 years – therefore, rarely. Usage: I like lobster, but it's too expensive to eat more than once in a blue moon.

TWO-FACED:

With two faces, a person could conceal one emotion while revealing another – therefore, to be hypocritical or deceitful. Usage: Some politicians are two-faced: They say one thing and do another.

Follow-ups:
1. Before or during a subsequent class, quickly sketch drawings that relate to the idioms you want the class to review and ask students to label them.
2. For homework or an ongoing project, have students collect new idioms of these types, write their meanings in a journal, draw, and label them.

   Have students share their idioms by circulating their journals to the class or to their group, or select idioms from the journals for students to present on the board.

Comments: Although idioms are informal uses of language, much more common in speech than in writing, and almost always avoided in academic work, they are important because their use in social settings helps establish a feeling of equality and unity between and among people.

A.1.22 Do or make?

Procedure: At the top of the board write *do* and *make*.

Ask students to tell you as many things they can that we *do* and list them in the *do* column. Repeat the process for things we *make*. Then add examples you can think of.

Ask students to work at their desks and sketch illustrations for the items on the lists. Then circulate, and choose students to draw their illustrations on the board.

Examples:

Do	Make
the dishes	our bed
homework	a phone call
housework or the cleaning	a list
our hair	dinner
our nails or our makeup	friends
the laundry or the washing	plans
ironing	a reservation
exercises	a face
the shopping	a mistake
research	war or peace
good (things)	changes or renovations
the decorating	additions or deletions
	money
	a mess
	a decision

Follow-ups:

1. Have students (at their desks) write sentences using the expressions they didn't know. Have some students write their sentences on the board.
2. To review at a later date, write the items from the two lists randomly over the board. Have students take turns going to the board and, with a different color of chalk or marker, write the correct verb next to one of the appropriate words or phrases.

Things we *do*:

our <u>homework</u>   the <u>laundry</u> or <u>washing</u>

our <u>hair</u>

our <u>nails</u>

Things we <u>make</u>:

our <u>bed</u>   a <u>phone call</u>   a <u>list</u>

A.1.23 Homonyms

Words that are pronounced the same but spelled differently, also known as *homophones*.

Procedure: To present and/or to practice homonyms, draw a rectangle on the board and divide it into four equal parts

Write one of a pair of homonyms in the top left box. Ask students for a synonym or brief definition and write it in the top right box. If students don't know what the word means, supply the meaning yourself and write it there.

Then ask for a word that sounds the same but is spelled differently. Write it in the lower left box.

Repeat the process for the definition of the homonym and write it in the lower right box.

Present a small number of different sets of homonyms – perhaps three sets if the concept is new to your students. For more advanced learners, you might present six or so sets.

Examples:

pain	a hurt
pane	a piece of glass

sun	source of daylight
son	mother's boy

new	not old
knew	past tense of know

When you have presented all the sets you want to cover, erase the homonyms and their definitions, keeping the boxes. Using a different order from the order in which you listed the sets of homonyms, fill in only the left-hand boxes – that is, write only the homonyms. Ask students to reconstruct the definitions or give new, correct ones if they can.

Follow-up: Before or during a subsequent class, again draw the rectangles and their divisions. Fill in the right-hand boxes with the definitions. Ask students to fill in the homonyms.

Once students understand what homonyms are, ask them to collect some new ones, perhaps asking native speakers or more advanced students to help.

Have your students bring the new homonyms to class and present them on the board in the same manner.

Comments: Students will often know one half of a homonym pair and learn a new word when they meet its partner: For example, they may know *pain* but not *pane*, *rain* but not *reign* (or *rein*), *main* but not *mane*. Other pairs to consider using are *break/brake*, *ring/wring*, *seen/scene*, *pray/prey*, *way/weigh*, *wait/weight*, *horse/hoarse*.

Homonym study also helps with pronunciation.

A.1.24 Reviewing and assessing new vocabulary

Preparation: Using recently introduced words (or words appearing in recent assignments that were new to a number of your students), design review exercises that can be done on the board.

Procedure: Permit students to write answers to exercises on the board randomly as they are able. This encourages spontaneous participation.

Or call on volunteers individually but allow them to provide answers to any question on the board. This avoids making students feel that the activity is a test rather than a review.

The following types of vocabulary review exercises can be used:

- *Scrambled Words:* Examples are cleets (select), esate (tease), vanaced (advance), and so on.
- *Missing Letters:* List some new words, leaving out one or two letters.

Variation: Scatter the words with missing letters over the board.

Divide the class into two teams, each with a captain to do the board work. Give each captain a chalk or marker different in color from the words on the board and different from each other's.

See which team can fill in the most missing letters.

- *Word Search:*

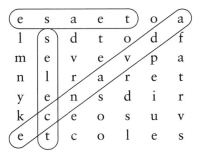

The level of difficulty can be adjusted by (1) avoiding or including answers written upside-down or backward, (2) by listing the words students are to find, (3) giving students a list of synonyms or other clues related to the words they are to find, or (4) telling students how many words are concealed and what the theme of the puzzle is.

- *Matching:*

_____ select	a. make fun of
_____ tease	b. move forward
_____ advance	c. choose

Follow-up: After this exercise has been completed, erase either the target words or the matching synonyms. Later in the class challenge students to remember what has been erased.

Variation: Have students match antonyms instead of synonyms.

- *Translation* (for EFL students): List words for students to translate either into or from their first language.
- *Odd Word Out:* Have students strike out or erase the word that doesn't belong:

select
a. choose
b. pick out
c. ~~change~~

Follow-up: After this exercise has been completed, erase the target words and the incorrect ("odd word") answers, leaving only the synonyms. Later in the class challenge students to recall the target words.

Homework or in-class follow-ups: As a homework assignment, have each student construct one of these exercises using the target words, for the class or for another student to do.

For in-class follow-up, divide the class into several small groups. Have each group construct an exercise for another group to do.

Consider having students write their exercises on the board. Public writing focuses attention on the students as "teachers" and on the activity in a way that paper handouts do not.

Comments: Scrambled words and word search are good warm-up activities to bring target words to mind and to reinforce spelling and syllabication. Use Matching for words students need in their active (speaking or writing) vocabulary. For words students need in their passive (listening or reading) vocabulary, use Odd Word Out.

A.1.25 More reviewing and assessing of new vocabulary

Procedure: Write a list of new vocabulary on the board, leaving sufficient space around and between each word to do additional writing.

Point to a word and ask students to provide information such as:

- What part of speech (word form) is this?
- What is another form of this word? (If it's a noun, ask for the adjective.)

As the students answer, write, or have a scribe write, the information next to the word.

Follow-ups:

1. To review new words and to expand students' understanding of the words, ask:

   - What is a synonym for this word?
   - What is the opposite of this word?

   Write these words next to the new word and connect them to the original word with radiating lines.

2. Have students review all of the base words and then ask them questions such as:

   - Which words have a positive or a negative connotation?
   - Which words can be used with people?
   - Which words can be used with things?
   - Which words are slang?

   Use a different color of chalk or marker for each of these questions, and use one color to circle all words that have the same characteristics. Provide a key if you wish; for example, write *people* in red and use red to circle the words that can be used with people.

3. Ask students:

   - Which word means _____?
   - Which word can be used to fill in the blank in this sentence? The _____ is empty.

4. Ask students to give a sentence using _____.
   Write these sample sentences on the board under the word.

A.1.26 Vocabulary stepping-stones

Reviewing the spelling of new words or recalling new words from their definitions.

Procedure: Draw a river with stepping-stones crossing it – one stone for each word that needs to be reviewed. To practice spelling, call out the word, and when a student spells it correctly, write the word on the stone.

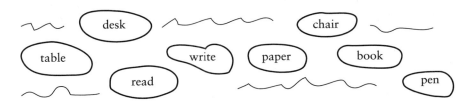

To review the meaning of new words, call out a definition: Students must name the word and spell it, whereupon you write it on a stone or the student comes forward and writes it. Continue until the class has crossed the river!

Variation: If your students like competitive games, divide the class into two teams and draw two sets of stepping-stones, perhaps allowing team scribes to do the board work. Teams lose their turn if they make an error.

Comment: If you have limited board space, work vertically by drawing ladders instead of stepping stones and entering words on the rungs.

Acknowledgment: This activity is based on one by W. R. Lee in *Language Teaching Games and Contests* (1987).

A.1.27 Do you remember?

Reviewing new vocabulary (a board version of what is commonly known as *Kim's game*).

Procedure: On the board write ten or twelve vocabulary words your class has been working on.

Give students a few minutes to look over the list, and then erase it or cover it with a sheet of newsprint or old newspaper.

Ask students (at their desks) to write down all the words they can remember. (Spelling counts!)

After a few minutes, rewrite or reveal the list so that students can check and correct or add missing words if necessary.

Variation: Before the final step of revealing the list, have students collaborate in pairs or groups of three to make a composite list and to try to remember more of the words.

Comment: A flip chart or an overhead projector works especially well for this activity.

A.1.28 Vocabulary ticktacktoe

Reviewing new words for meaning and/or for spelling.

Preparation: Select a number of words that your students are working with. These can be vocabulary words you want the students to remember the meaning of, or words they already know but find difficult to spell.

Procedure for vocabulary review: Briefly review the selected words with your class.

Then draw a ticktacktoe grid on the board.

Divide students into two teams and have each team select a scribe.

In order to earn an X or an O on the grid, a team member must first correctly answer a question you ask, such as: "What word means the same as _____ ?" or "Which of our new words is missing from this sentence: 'The hen sat on her eggs until they _____ .'"?

The scribe chooses a team member to answer the question and enters his or her team's symbol (i.e., an X or an O) on the grid if the answer is correct.

Variation: Proceed as above, but the chosen team member must use the word correctly in a sentence.

If you wish, writing the sentence on the board, with help from team members, can also be part of the scribe's duties.

Procedure for spelling review: Draw a *large* ticktacktoe grid. Assign each team different colored chalk or markers. Pronounce one of the words to be practiced, but instead of having a scribe enter an X or an O, call on individual team members to go to the board and write the spelling word in the box of their choice. If it is correct, it remains; if it is incorrect, erase it and give the word to the opposing team. The team that first completes a row of words written in its color wins.

A.1.29 Blankety-blank

Based on the TV game *Wheel of Fortune.*

Procedure: Choose the name of a person, place, or thing or a phrase (phrasal verbs or idioms work well). On the board draw a blank for each letter in the word(s) you've chosen and underneath write the name of the applicable category:

Example:

— — — — — — —

PLACE

(Answer: airport)

Students take turns guessing what letters might appear in the mystery word(s). A correct guess of *a consonant* earns 5 points for each time the letter occurs. Therefore, a player guessing *r* in response to the example above would earn 10 points. Vowels must be bought, however; and *each vowel* costs 2 points. Keep track of players' names and scores on the board.

If consonants guessed or vowels bought are contained in the mystery word(s), the player's score is calculated and the player gets another turn. If the guess is incorrect, the player loses his or her turn.

Players can guess the solution after making a correct letter guess, or they can guess the solution instead of guessing a letter, but an incorrect solution costs them their turn.

Follow-up: Permit the winning student to choose the mystery word(s) and do the board writing.

Variation for large classes: Divide the class into two or three teams.

A.1.30   Make a new word

Preparation: Make a list of a number of words (as in the examples in this activity) that will form other words when a letter is added.

Procedure: Have three or four students go to the board; allow enough room for each student to work comfortably. Have students at their seats work on paper.

Spell out the base word, and define the word if you think that your students may not be familiar with it. Then instruct them to add a letter, but do not tell them what the letter should be. Also, give them a definition of the target word. For example, give them *rob* as a base word, and tell them to add a letter to make something worn over pajamas (*robe*).

Give beginning-level students base words that make a new word when the letter is added at the end, as in examples 1 to 4 on the next page. Intermediate-level students may add letters at the end or at the beginning, as in examples 5 to 7. Have advanced students add medial letters as well, as in the remaining examples.

Keep score. The first student at the board to get five correct answers gets to play again. The others choose a classmate to replace them. Play until all students have had a chance to write at the board. If time permits and your list holds out, have a winners' play-off.

Examples:

Base word	+ add a letter =	Target word
rob	worn over pajamas =	1. robe
car		2. card
hear		3. heart
dance		4. dancer
lap		5. slap
mile		6. smile
late		7. plate
though		8. through
cap		9. clap
sow		10. show

Variation: Note that the categories can be reversed. Give them *robe,* ask
them to erase a letter to make a synonym for *steal* (rob), and so on:

tent	ten
cute	cut
ripe	rip
hate	hat
glove	love
chair	hair
fact	act
ago	go
price	rice
boat	bat
stocks	socks
steep	step

Follow-up: As students become familiar with the activity, beginners and
intermediates may be able to take on the next level of difficulty. Also,
students at advanced levels may want to design their own lists and lead
the activity.

A.1.31 Playing with words

Procedure: Divide your class into teams, and have the groups work at their desks on one of the challenges that follow:

1. Challenge teams to see how many words they can write that:

   - Begin with a specific letter.
   - End with a specific letter.
   - Begin or end with a specific prefix or suffix.
   - Contain seven (or more) letters.
   - Belong in a specific domain (e.g., animals, foods, professions, colors – for lower level students; illnesses, courses of study, emotions – for higher levels).
   - Contain double letters.

2. Write a new vocabulary word on the board and see which team can make the most words out of it (e.g., *tentative* contains *ant, native, teen, in, even, vein,* and at least two dozen more words).

   Set a time limit of 10 to 15 minutes, which you can, of course, extend if all the teams want to keep working when time is up. Then have the teams count their answers. Have the team that has the most answers send a scribe to the board to record them so that the others can add examples from their lists that the winning team may lack and all students can have an opportunity to question words on the board whose meanings they don't know.

   If you want more students to do the public writing, send a scribe from each team to the board to display his or her team's list to determine which team has the greatest number of different answers.

Variations for advanced learners:

1. Challenge teams to see which team can come up with an example of a double-letter word for each letter of the alphabet, with the exception of *j, q, x,* and *y,* which do not appear doubled in English words. You might also want to omit *vv,* which does appear in *flivver* but is a word even few native speakers know.

   More common words that contain double letters in English include *bazaar, rubbish, accept, address, been, office, luggage, skiing, bookkeeper, hill, mommy, nanny, loop, poppy, hurry, sassy, better, vacuum, powwow,* and *snazzy.*

2. Challenge teams to find words that are palindromes (words spelled the same forward and backward), for example, *bib, civic, did, eye, gag, level, mom, noon, peep, refer, sis, tot,* and *wow.*

3. Challenge teams to find words that contain various combinations of vowels such as *ao* (*chaos, aorta*), *iu* (*genius*), *io* (*lion, prior*), *oe* (*goes, does*), *eo* (*reoccur*), *uo* (*quote, quota, continuous*) and combinations

of consonants such as *nw* (*inward*), *mf* (*comfort*), *dm* (*handmade*), *lv* (*halves, themselves*), *nj* (*enjoy*), *pt* (*empty*), and *nm* (*inmate, inmost*).

Acknowledgment: Activities for advanced learners in this activity are based on some described by Dwight Spenser in *Word Games in English*, (1976).

A.2 Pronunciation

Use of the board can help us teach pronunciation if we draw illustrations of mouth positions and phonetic symbols as well as marks showing stress and intonation. We can also use the board to indicate elision. In the next activities, which illustrate these subjects, I have used the graphics I normally use in the classroom.

For additional models for drawing mouth positions, see, for example, Linda Lane, *Focus on Pronunciation: Principles and Practice for Effective Communications* (1993).

For phonetic symbols or rules and principles of stress and intonation for American English, see, for example, Rebecca M. Dauer, *Accurate English: A Complete Course in Pronunciation* (1993), Stacy A. Hagen and Patricia E. Grogan, *Sound Advantage: A Pronunciation Book* (1992), or Linda Grant, *Well Said: Advanced English Pronunciation* (1993).

For British English, see Heinz J. Giegerich, *English Phonology: An Introduction* (1992).

Another way we can use the board in teaching pronunciation is to show students that English words that look as if they would be pronounced the same way may not be, and that words that look as if they would be pronounced differently from each other may, in fact, be pronounced the same! Activity A.2.3 is a prime example, and several subsequent activities can be used to illustrate this point as well.

Although the activities in this section focus primarily on these two ways of using the board to teach pronunciation, they are not intended to cover all aspects of either subject, nor is the section as a whole intended to provide comprehensive coverage of all aspects of learning how to speak English.

A.2.1 Basic features of English pronunciation
A.2.2 Practicing stress patterns
A.2.3 Sight and sound: Same or different?
A.2.4 Does it rhyme?
A.2.5 Words that begin with _____
A.2.6 *th* voiced /ð/ and *th* voiceless /θ/
A.2.7 Numbers ending in *-teen* and those ending in *-ty*
A.2.8 Verbs with *-ed* endings
A.2.9 Multiple-syllable homographs

Language-based activities

See also:

A.2.1 Basic features of English pronunciation

Presenting and practicing phonetics, elision, stress, and intonation.

PHONETICS

Procedure: On the board, draw positions of the mouth, tongue, and lips
to show students where sounds are made:

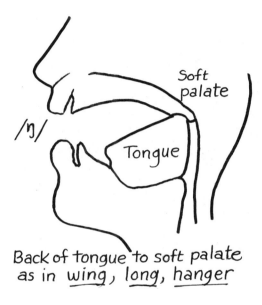

Back of tongue to soft palate
as in wing, long, hanger

ELISION

Procedure: Write pairs of words, phrases, or complete sentences on the
board and draw lines connecting final sounds and initial sounds that
are commonly run together in normal speech, for example:

left town
talks slowly
Where can I get tickets to the big game?

With an eraser, illustrate elisions that form contractions:

How is your mother?   How s your mother?   How's your mother?
I did not hear you.   I did n t hear you.   I didn't hear you.

STRESS AND INTONATION

Procedure: Write a sentence on the board, and mark it using your favorite
method of indicating stress.

I mark both stressed and unstressed words and syllables, and I underline the word that represents the information focus. Therefore, a marked sentence would look like this:

Hów dŏ ўou <u>feél</u> now?

For intonation, I draw a line with an arrow above the sentence, tracing the rising and falling pitch of the human voice:

Where is the cafeteria?

Follow-up: On the board, write new examples of pairs of words or phrases that elide and ask students to mark them using your method of indicating their pronunciation. Do the same with sentences to be marked for stress and intonation.

Comment: There are many methods that can be used to indicate stress and intonation. If you don't already have a favorite method, use the one illustrated above or consider one of the following:

- Use capital letters or accent marks to illustrate the stressed syllables or words, and mark unstressed syllables or words or simply leave them unadorned:

  EMphasis or emphăsĭs or merely emphasis.

- Place a bullet over the information focus instead of underlining it:

  "How is your mother?"

- Use large letters or leave spaces to illustrate differences in stress patterns and vowel quality:

  f i f t e e n   f i f t y

  m a n   men

  s h e e p   ship

Acknowledgment: The last three examples are from John Yates, "Using the Blackboard" (1981).

A.2.2 Practicing stress patterns

Preparation: Prepare a list of questions, such as those shown below, together with a list of responses. Write them on the board in two columns. To begin, mark the stress and information focus as in the examples, as long as you think that your students need them:

A	B
1. Whát tíme ăre ýou ărríviňg?	a. Ĕlévĕn ŏ'clóck.
2. Whát tíme dĭd yŏu śay yŏu wŏuld ărríve?	b. I sáid ĕlévĕn ŏ'clóck.
3. Whóse bŏok iš thát?	c. Thăt's Jóhn's bŏok.
4. Whích bŏok iš Jóhn's?	d. Thát's Jŏhn's bŏok.
5. Trý tŏ rĕmémbĕr thĕ númbĕr.	e. Ĭ ám trýiňg.
6. Dŏ yŏu rĕmémbĕr thĕ númbĕr?	f. I'm trýiňg.
7. Whŏ knóws thĕ ańsŵer?	g. Í dŏ.
8. Dŏ ýou knŏw the ánsŵer?	h. Ĭ dó.

Procedure: Read an entry from column A, and invite a student to read the matching column B entry using the indicated inflection.

Comment: Students will need time to read the possible responses silently and to decide on the correct inflection. Students who are practicing this type of material for the first time may need you to read both the A prompt and the B response, and then they may need to echo the response before they are able to respond on their own.

Follow-ups:

1. Have students work in pairs, taking turns reading the questions and answers.
2. Have pairs of students write their own pairs of examples and take turns reading them.
3. Select some of the best student examples for display on the board and public reading.

A.2.3   Sight and sound: Same or different?

Procedure: On the board write a number of pairs of words whose spelling makes them look as if their vowels (and sometimes their consonant combinations) would be pronounced the same but actually are not pronounced the same, and write some that look as if their vowels (and sometimes consonant combinations) would be pronounced differently but are actually pronounced the same.

Examples:

A.	moth/both	N.	oak/smoke
B.	moth/mother	O.	guess/yes
C.	both/bother	P.	please/pleasure
D.	brother/bother	Q.	scare/are
E.	road/rode	R.	quit/suit
F.	thing/think	S.	floor/four
G.	bead/head	T.	by/buy
H.	seem/team	U.	straight/eight
I.	sowed/toad	V.	vein/vane
J.	cool/food	W.	zoo/to
K.	now/know	X.	toe/go
L.	bed/dead	Y.	heart/part
M.	dumb/some	Z.	main/mane

Establish codes or symbols; for example, you could use an *S* for *same* or *D* for *different,* or an = sign for *same* and ≠ for *different.* Begin by pronouncing a pair of words and asking students to determine which code or symbol should be written next to the words.

Once the list is complete, thoroughly erase the symbols that have been assigned and call on students to pronounce the pairs, telling you or a scribe which symbols or codes to write next to the word pairs.

Acknowledgment: This activity is based on one in Helene D. Hutchinson, *ESL Teacher's Book of Instant Word Games for Grades 7–12* (1997), but adults can benefit from and enjoy it, too.

A.2.4   Does it rhyme?

Linking the pronunciation of new words to known words through rhyme.

Procedure: On the board write new vocabulary words that students are working on, leaving room between the words for students to stand comfortably to write. Assign one new word to each student unless you have more students than new words, in which case have students work in pairs; or have some students work at their desks, suggesting additional words to the board writers and acting as editors when the board writing is complete.

Ask students to write as many words as they already know that rhyme with the new word they have been assigned.

When students are "finished," point out or have student editors point out any words that do not rhyme with the new vocabulary word.

Also, have students ask their peers for definitions of rhyming words they don't know.

Comment: A by-product of this activity is that you and the students will discover and can correct some of their misconceptions about what words sound the same as the target words.

A.2.5 Words that begin with _____

Procedure: Pick a letter or letters that represent a sound that some or all of your students have difficulty pronouncing when it is used at the beginning of a word.

Ask students to contribute words that begin with the initial sound. Write, or have a student write, each new word on the board.

When the list is complete, have students take turns reading it. If the list is long, have each student read only the words she or he contributed.

Variation: Pick an adjective that begins with the sound you want your students to practice. Ask students to contribute nouns that can logically follow that adjective and that begin with the same sound as the adjective. For example, if you want them to practice pronouncing initial *l-*, give them the adjective *lovely* or *loud*. A student might then supply an answer such as *lovely lady* or *loud laugh*. For *r-*, give them *red*, or *round*, or *rough*. For *th-*, use *thick* or *thin; y-, young* or *yellow; h-, heavy* or *hard*.

Be sure that students repeat the adjective along with the noun they supply.

Write each response on the board so that students can practice by repeating.

Comment: This is a good warm-up or wind-down activity.

A.2.6 *th* voiced /ð/ and *th* voiceless /θ/

Preparation: You may want to present the concepts *voiced* and *voiceless* before beginning this activity.

Procedure: Using a wide expanse of board and one color of chalk or marker, write a number of examples of words that contain the consonant combination *th*. Some of the words should be examples of *th* when it is voiced, as in *then* and *rather,* and some should be examples of voiceless *th,* as in *think* and *both,* as shown below:

m	wealthy	f		other
a		a		
t		t	thin	
h		h		
	the	e		health
	thirteenth	r		

Then divide students into two teams, each with a captain to work at the board. Give each captain a colored chalk or marker that is different in color from the other captain's and different from the one you used.

Announce that the goal will be to locate and circle all of the words in which the letters *th* are either voiced or voiceless, as you prefer.

When both sides believe that there are no more words left to circle, count up correct answers for each side and point out any incorrect answers by modeling the correct pronunciation.

Follow-up: Later, or in a subsequent class, divide an expanse of board into two sections. Write the phonetic symbol for voiced *th* (/ð/) at the top of one section and the symbol for voiceless *th* (/θ/) at the top of the other.

Divide the class into two teams, and assign one team to each column.

The goal is to find out which team can come up with the most words in which *th* begins or ends a word or appears within the word and that fit the pronunciation the team has been assigned.

Comment: Note that in general the *th* sound in grammatical items such as *the, this, neither,* and *whether* is voiced but in lexical items it is either voiced or voiceless.

A.2.7 Numbers ending in *-teen* and those ending in *-ty*

Preparation: You will need fifteen slips of paper, each bearing one of these numbers: 13, 14, 15, 16, 17, 18, 19, 20, 30, 40, 50, 60, 70, 80, 90. Put the slips in a hat or bowl.

Procedure: Write the numbers on the board and explain to students that they can distinguish the numbers ending in *-teen* from those ending in *-ty* by:

- Stress, since we accent *-teen* but not *-ty*.
- The length of the syllable, since *-teen* is usually drawn out whereas *-ty* is usually pronounced quickly.
- The final *n* in *-teen* (to some extent), especially when it precedes a word that begins with a vowel.

Model the pronunciation and give students opportunities to practice.

Next, divide the class into two or more teams, each with a captain to do the boardwork. For *each* team, draw a grid on the board like these:

13	15	19		17	40	30
60	40	18		14	13	70
80	17	30		16	90	50

Write some *-teen* numbers and some *-ty* numbers in the grids. Some numbers can appear on more than one grid, but no three numbers in a row should be the same (or two teams could be winners).

Draw the prepared slips of paper with the numbers written on them from the hat or bowl and announce them one by one.

Captains should circle each number you call that is on their grid. Colored chalk or markers work well for this activity.

The first team to get three numbers in a row – up, down, or slantwise – wins.

Variations: Prepare slips of papers and grids with dates that include *-teens* and *-tys* (such as 1990/1919, 1712/1730), with times (10:15/10:50, 1:13/1:30), or with prices ($3.30/$3.13, £14.40/£14.14).

Examples:

1990	1960	1817		1870	1919	1980
1814	1919	1980		1915	1840	1770
1950	1730	1918		1817	1713	1816

10:15	11:13	1:30		7:15	9:30	12:50
6:30	12:15	8:15		10:50	11:30	1:15
7:50	1:13	4:50		6:13	4:15	8:50

$3.30	$18.50	$8.15		$3.13	$2.40	$12.15
$14.40	$12.50	$3.13		$14.14	$17.90	$8.50
$70.19	$19.80	$12.15		$2.14	$19.18	$12.50

£13.30	£18.50	£8.15		£13.13	£22.40	£12.15
£15.50	£12.50	£33.13		£15.15	£17.90	£98.50
£70.19	£19.80	£12.15		£42.14	£19.18	£12.50

A.2.8 Verbs with *-ed* endings

Preparation: You may want to present the concepts *voiced* and *voiceless* before beginning this activity.

Procedure: Draw three columns on the board, each headed by one of the possible pronunciations of final *-ed*.

Ask students to name some regular verbs. Ask them to pronounce the verb in the past tense and to tell you in which column to enter the verb. If they cannot tell you which column, pronounce the verb in the past tense to find out whether they can hear the ending.

Example:

-ed /əd/	-ed /t/	-ed /d/
ended	kissed	called
hated	hoped	played

When you have gathered a sufficient number of examples, ask students to work with a partner or in small groups to determine the rule for each of the differently pronounced endings.

Have winning students write their rule(s) on the board.

Rules should go basically like this: Final -*ed* following a /t/ or /d/ sound is pronounced as a separate syllable: /əd/. Final -*ed* following a voiceless consonant other than /t/ is pronounced /t/. Final -*ed* following a vowel or voiced consonant other than /d/ is pronounced /d/.

Follow-up: Using a wide expanse of board and one color of chalk or marker, write a number of regular past tense verbs at random:

```
          called    w              s
      d             a              h
    e               i    stayed    i
    g               t  l           p      washed
  d       picked    e    a         p
  u               d     n    d     e
j                           e      d
                               d   d
```

Divide students into three teams, each with a captain to do the work at the board (with verbal help from their teammates). Give each captain chalk or a marker different in color from the one you used and from the other's.

Assign one verb ending (/t/, or /d/, or /əd/) to each captain and explain that the goal is for each captain to locate and circle all the verbs whose ending he or she has been assigned.

When the captains believe that they have no more words left to circle, count up the correct answers for each team and point out any incorrect answers by modeling the correct pronunciation.

Variation: Use the same procedure to present and practice rules for pronunciation of words when -*s* is added to form a plural, a third person singular present tense verb, or the possessive case:

-*s* /əz/	-*s* /z/	-*s* /s/
judges	cars	books
churches	drives	waits

Students should produce rules that go basically like this: Final -*s* following voiceless /s/, /š/, and /č/ or voiced /z/, /ž/, and /ǰ/ is pronounced as a separate syllable, either /əz/ or /ɪz/. Following any voiceless sound other than /s/, /š/, or /č/, it is pronounced /s/. Following any voiced sound other than /z/, /ž/ or /ǰ/, it is pronounced /z/.

Comment: To keep students focused on improving their ability to employ the correct -*ed* or final -*s* pronunciation, use Activity A.7.1, Targeting correct language use: Vocabulary, pronunciation, or grammar.

A.2.9 Multiple-syllable homographs

Using examples to formulate a rule for pronouncing "true" multiple-syllable homographs (words that are spelled the same but pronounced differently).

Procedure: Draw a grid on the board like the one on the next page.

1. Explain to students that true homographs are words that are (a) spelled the same but pronounced differently and that are (b) not related in meaning.

   Students should also know that, although there are not a lot of true homographs, several pairs of them are important and frequently used words of which they should be aware in order to avoid confusion – both in pronouncing and in understanding them. Fortunately, there is a rule for pronouncing most multiple-syllable homographs that you can help them formulate.

	Stress first syllable	Stress second syllable
content (n.)	n.	
content (v. or adj.)		v. or adj.
desert (n.)		
desert (v.)		
entrance (n.)		
entrance (v.)		
invalid (n.)		
invalid (adj.)		
object (n.)		
object (v.)		
project (n.)		
project (v.)		
refuse (n.)		
refuse (v.)		

2. Before moving on to pronunciation, be sure that students know the meaning of the listed homographs. One way to be sure is to ask students for synonyms or short definitions or to supply them yourself for any words the students do not already know. You may also wish to write the synonyms or definitions on the board.

3. Begin your search for the rule of pronouncing multiple-syllable homographs by pronouncing each pair and asking students to listen for the difference in stress. Have them tell you in which column to enter *n.* and in which column to enter *v.* and/or *adj.* (*content* has been done as an example).

4. When all the words have been processed, ask students (a) to formulate the rule for pronouncing multiple-syllable homographs and (b) to tell you, if they can, what additional differences in pronunciation they hear.

   They should have no trouble telling from the chart they develop that the stress is usually on the first syllable in nouns and on the second syllable in verbs and adjectives. But they might need a little help in understanding that the vowel quality also changes when a syllable is unstressed; that is, it is reduced, and the time it takes to say it is shortened. Therefore, you may have to accentuate these differences for them.

Variation: You may want to also deal with multiple-syllable homographs that follow the same pronunciation rule as that described above but *are* related in meaning, such as *compound, convict, extract, insult, perfect, permit, present, progress, record, subject,* and *survey.*

A.3 Grammar

When you introduce new grammatical structures or new activities, it is best to start by using a short, simple model. More complex grammar may be targeted if you have high intermediate or advanced students after they understand the basic principles.

Also, involving students actively and publicly in practicing new grammatical structures helps them absorb and retain the material. In addition, this practice allows you to assess how well and by whom the material is being learned.

The grammatical constructions covered in this section focus on verb tenses, word forms, sentence construction, and/or syntax. This section is not intended to provide comprehensive coverage of all grammatical structures in English.

Language-based activities

See also:

A.3.1   Verb tenses: Simple present

Procedure: Write a list of verbs in the simple present tense on the board, such as:

drive	am/is/are
live	love
have/has	hate
own	

Draw some pictures of items on the board that can be subjects or objects of these verbs, such as those on the next page.

Have students create sentences to describe the pictures using the verbs in the simple present tense.

Examples:

1. My father drives (or owns or has) a car.
2. The boy has a ball. The children have a ball. The children are playing.
3. I am afraid of storms.
4. I hate snakes.
5. I have three dollars and 50 cents. (I have two pounds and 70 shillings.)
6. I love flowers.
7. Mrs. Rodgers owns (or lives in or has) a house. People live in houses.

Students can contribute sentences orally, or they can dictate sentences for you to write on the board, or they can write the sentences there themselves.

Follow-ups:

1. Have students use more than one verb when possible (see Examples 1 and 7).
2. Have them practice constructing their sentences using both singular and plural subjects or objects (see Examples 2 and 7).

A.3.2 Verb tenses: Present, past, and future

Procedure: Divide your class into teams of three to five members each and mark off a space at the board for each team.

Explain that the object is for one member from each team to write a sentence on the board that fulfills the requirements that you will announce. Each team member should have a turn to write on the board. Other members can verbally help the writer, but they may not write down the sentence on paper for the purpose of having it copied onto the board.

Next, announce the requirements for the sentence: the gender and number of its subject, the activity the subject is doing, and the time.

Example: You might say that the subject is *one male,* the verb is *to drive,* and the time is *the future.* A student might then write: "He will drive his car to work tomorrow" or "Michael will drive a big car someday." You can give points for correctness, originality, level of difficulty, or other criteria if you wish.

Acknowledgment: This activity is based on one by Nanette Woonton, "Dave's ESL Cafe: Dave's ESL Idea Page." <www.eslcafe.com> (June 15, 1998).

A.3.3 Verb tenses: Present, past, and future (of *to be*); present perfect and present perfect progressive

Procedure: Draw a horizontal line on the board and place a vertical line through its center. Explain to students that the horizontal line represents time and the vertical line is the present.

Write a sentence in the present tense above the line, and draw an illustration of the sentence on the line at the vertical mark:

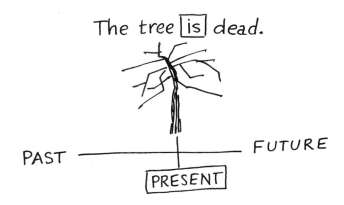

Follow the same procedure for the past and future tenses:

The tree [was] green last summer.

[PAST] ———————|——————— FUTURE

PRESENT

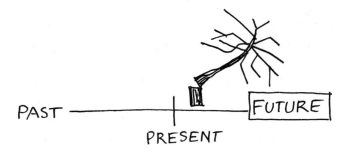

The tree [will be] cut down tomorrow.

PAST ——————|——— [FUTURE]

PRESENT

Write other sentences and draw other illustrations if needed.

When students have grasped the concept, erase the sentences, leaving only the time lines and the verbs.

Then ask students to restore the missing sentences.

Finally, have students suggest other sentences using the verbs, and write these sentences on the board for students to copy into their notebooks.

Homework: Have students compose additional sentences for use on the board.

Variations: You can use the same format to present other tenses, for example, the present perfect:

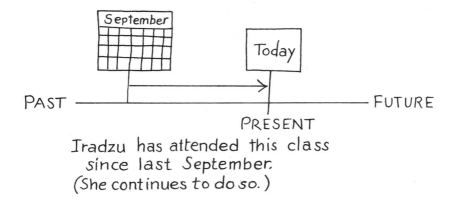

Iradzu has attended this class
since last September.
(She continues to do so.)

The present perfect progressive can be illustrated like this:

This class has been meeting
for 3 months.

Follow-up: Ask students questions about their lives and use their responses to create more examples; for example, "How long have you lived here?" "How long have you been studying English?"

A.3.4 Reviewing verb tenses

Procedure: Draw the chart below on the board. Across the top, label each
  column with the tense you want the students to use. In the first column,
  write the person and the verbs you want the students to use.

  Either call on students by name or ask for volunteers to fill in the
  remaining squares.

  Enter their answers yourself or have students come to the board to
  do their own writing.

Example:

Person / Verb	Present	Past	Present perfect
Second singular / talk			
First singular / sing			
Third singular / be			
Third plural / go			

Variations: You can use similar charts to practice other aspects of verbs.

Additional examples:

Person Verb/tense	Affirmative	Negative
First singular go/present		
Third singular put/present progressive		
First plural walk/present perfect		
Third plural watch/present perfect progressive		

Verb/tense	Active	Passive
prepare/past		
take/present		
blame/future		
cook/present perfect		

Person Verb/tense	Statement	Question	Command
Second singular call/present			
Third plural imagine/past			
First singular carry/future			
First plural fix/present perfect			

Comment: Making this work public provides opportunities for peer tutoring and ensures that students have correct models to copy into their notebooks. In addition, it gives you the ability to monitor students as they work and the option of intervening at the moment problems occur.

Follow-up: On a sheet of paper, draw the chart your students need to practice. Add the person and verbs that are most difficult for your students to master. Duplicate the chart and use it as homework.

A.3.5 More reviewing of verb tenses

Changing verb tenses, person, voice, aspect, sentence structure; practicing special spelling rules.

Procedure: Ask several students to write a sentence on the board using a regular verb in the present tense and active voice. Begin by giving all the students the same verb and person. You may want to choose verbs that need to be practiced.

Then have each student (1) change places with another student already at the board and (2) change that student's sentence to the past tense.

Students at their seats can be doing the same activity on paper and exchanging papers with other seated students, and they can also be called upon to edit or help with board writing.

After students see how the activity works, have those at the board change places with seated students.

This time, assign each student at the board a different verb, but you might want to give students all regular or all irregular verbs to keep the level of difficulty relatively equal. Allow students working at their seats to choose one of the assigned verbs to work with.

Repeat the initial procedure.

Variations: Use the same technique to practice:

- Changing verbs to the future or some other tense.
- Changing person.
- Changing voice (active or passive).
- Changing aspect (simple, perfect, progressive).
- Changing sentence structure (affirmative or negative, statement or question).
- Special spelling rules for regular verbs in the past tense such as *to marry, to supply, to study,* so that students can practice changing -*y* to -*i* + -*es* or -*i* + -*ed,* or *to shop, to plan, to bat,* so that they can practice doubling the final consonant.

Comment: This activity provides good opportunities for peer tutoring and ensures that students have correct models to copy into their notebooks.

In addition, you can monitor students as they work; and you can intervene, if you wish to, at the moment you see a problem occur.

A.3.6 There is . . ./there are; there was . . ./ there were . . .

Procedure: Write *there is* and *there are* on the board and explain that their function is (1) to call attention to the existence of something, or (2) to call attention to the location of something.

Draw a large picture frame on the board and draw an object in it, as shown on the next page. Keep the drawing simple.

Ask the students to use *there is* or *there are* to answer the question, "What is in the picture?"

Example:
    T: "What is in the picture?" S: "*There is* a tree in the picture."
    Add a second tree to the illustration, and repeat the question.
    Draw other frames with single and multiple objects in them, and repeat the procedure.
    Students may need extra practice using *there is* or *there are* when the plurality isn't immediately obvious. Therefore, you may need to draw some frames with two different objects in them, as shown on the next page.

Example:
    T: "What is in the picture?" S: "*There are* a house and a tree in the picture."*
    When students have grasped the principle of using these forms in the present tense, introduce them in the past tense by drawing the frame with an object in it and then erasing the object. Ask: "What *was* in the picture?"
    When students have mastered the past tense, draw a larger frame with several single and multiple objects in it.
    Call on students to describe orally the object(s) that are in the frame.
    Then erase the objects and have students write a description of what *was* in the frame.

---

* Some teachers prefer to use the singular construction *there is* when there is more than one subject and the first subject is singular.

Ask students who have correct descriptions to write them on the board to provide model responses.

Follow-up: Have some students create some pictures on the board, and call on other students to describe them.

Comment: You can also use this activity to present and practice prepositions of place.

Since many speakers of other languages confuse *there is* and *it is* constructions, you may want to use the activity that follows in conjunction with this one. Also see Activities B.1.4 and B.3.3.

A.3.7 It is . . ./it was . . .

Procedure: Write *it is* on the board and explain that this construction functions as the subject and verb of a sentence describing

- Time
- Temperature
- Weather
- Distance
- An environmental fact that is geographical or physical

Begin by giving students one or two simple examples such as the clock and the thermometer illustrated on the next page.

Language-based activities

Label these drawings with the responses you will be seeking; for example, it is (current time), and it is 35 degrees.

After the students grasp the principle, continue with other examples but do not label them.

Examples:

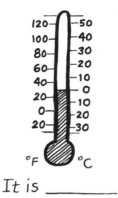

It is ____   It is _____

T: "What time is it?"   T: "How hot is it?"
S: "It is 12:30."   S: "It is 32 degrees Fahrenheit
                              (0 degrees Celsius)."

For weather, ask, "Is it raining?"

For distance, ask, "Is it far from A to B?"

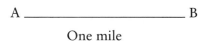

One mile

For an environmental fact (geographical) ask, "Is it mountainous in Chile?"

For an environmental fact (physical) ask, "Is it noisy at band practice?"

Follow-up: When students have grasped the principle of using *it is* in the present tense, introduce them to the past tense by erasing the hands on the clock. Ask, "What time was it?" And so on.

Comments:

1. Since *it's* is more commonly used in speech, you may want to use it throughout this activity.
2. Since many speakers of other languages confuse *it is* and *there is* constructions, you may want to use the preceding activity in conjunction with this one.

A.3.8 Modals: Possibility, obligation, and necessity

Procedure: Ask individuals or pairs or teams to prepare and make an oral presentation using the board as a visual aid to teach the basics of a game; for example, a sport such as baseball, soccer, or tennis; a board or card game such as Parcheesi, Monopoly, or Solitaire; a word game such as Scrabble or a game that is typical of your students' culture.

Suggest that they begin by brainstorming for vocabulary they will need to use and that they write words on the board that the audience will need to know.

Have them also draw on the board the playing field (the baseball diamond, for example, or the soccer field), the board (Monopoly, Parcheesi) or the layout (Solitaire), and any necessary equipment or accessories (balls, nets, dice).

Tell them to use the drawing to help explain the game and to use as many modals (*may, might, can, could, should, must, have to*) as possible in their explanation.

Example:

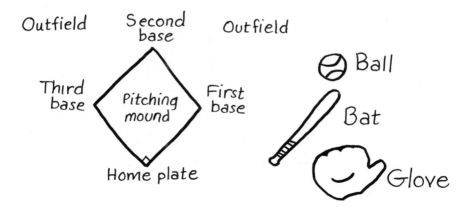

During the presentation, have students who are listening take notes of the rules for playing the game.

After the presentation, select several students to write on the board some of the rules from their notes, using complete sentences with modals.

Have the presenter correct any factual errors.

Work with the whole class to correct any errors in the modals.

Acknowledgment: This activity is based on one in Penny Ur, *Grammar Practice Activities: A Practical Guide for Teachers* (1988).

A.3.9 Question words

Procedure: Begin by drawing on the board the table shown here to help students see the basic pattern involved in *wh-* questions:

Question word	Helping verb	Subject	Main verb
Who (informal)	did	you	see?
Whom (formal)	did	you	see?
What	did	you	do?
Where	did	you	go?
When	did	you	leave?
Why	did	you	leave?

Then cue students with a question word and have them read the question. For example, you say, "What . . ." and they respond, "What did you do?"

When students can respond easily to the cues, have them work with a partner, taking turns asking the complete question and making up answers.

Next, erase all but the question words and have students repeat the last step.

Now have students repeat the activity, but have them change the subjects and verbs; for example, "Who(m) did he marry?" "Kirsten Murphy."

Finally, write a chart like this one on the board and have students supply the correct questions:

Q: A: At 9:30.	Q: A: George and Marcella.
Q: A: To Lefty's Pizza Parlor.	Q: A: Played Bingo.
Q: A: Because I was homesick.	

Comment: You may want to remind students that *wh-* words may also be the subject of sentences, as in "Who left?" or "What caused the problem?"

A.3.10   Copycat grammar

Modeling sentences with target grammar constructions for students to copy

Procedure: On the board write a sentence employing a target grammatical construction and draw a box around the word or phrase you want students to copy.
Example:

Who likes old movies?

Explain to students that they must use the same grammar used in your model sentence but all the words must be theirs except for the word or phrase in the box. In this case, then, their first word must be *Who,* the second word a main verb in the present tense, the third an adjective and the fourth a noun. (Students might write, "Who wants more homework?" or "Who hates rainy weather?")

Next, without checking for correct answers, call on some students to display their sentences on the board and ask those who did not write publicly to make any necessary corrections in the board examples.

Additional examples:

1. Don't go to bed mad! (Negative imperative)

2. There's a spider on your neck! (*There's a* construction)

3. An elephant is bigger than a peanut. (Comparison)

Acknowledgment: This activity is based on one in Mario Rinvolucri, *Grammar Games: Cognitive, Affective and Drama Activities for ESL Students* (1984).

A.3.11 What's different? Comparatives

Procedure: Choose a very simple object and draw two contrasting versions of it to illustrate differences such as bigger and smaller, longer or taller and shorter, wider and narrower, higher and lower, more and fewer, close and farther.

Draw the illustrations on the board, and ask students to describe the differences orally using comparisons. Then ask them to write sentences on the board under the illustrations to describe the differences.

Example:

The tree on the left is taller than the
tree on the right; the tree on the
right is shorter than the tree on the left.

Follow-ups: For homework, ask students to prepare some of their own illustrations demonstrating other comparisons such as older and younger, paler and darker, sooner and later.

Choose some students to draw their illustrations on the board; then ask each of them to choose a student who did not draw to write the comparison.

Variation: Follow the procedure above using three drawings to illustrate the use of superlatives.

A.3.12 Comparisons

Use of *the same (as), different (from),* and *similar (to).*

Procedure:

1. On the board write:

The same (as)	
1	2
B	B

Underneath write: *1 and 2 are the same.*

Read this statement to your students and have them repeat it in unison; then call on individual students to repeat it.

When this step has been mastered, write: *1 is the same as 2* under the first statement and repeat the procedure.

2. Next, use another chart to illustrate:

Different (from)	
3	4
M	V

3 and 4 are different.
3 is different from 4.

Then repeat as in item 1.

3. Then, use another chart to illustrate:

Similar (to)	
5	6
O	Q

5 and 6 are similar.
5 is similar to 6.
   Again, repeat as in item 1.
Follow-up: On the board, make a chart as follows:

1	2	3	4	5	6	7	8
L	O	Q	X	L	E	X	F

   Next, model a few sentences for students such as:

1 and 5 are the same.
3 is different from 6.
6 and 8 are similar.

   Have a number of students go to the board.
   Call out two numbers in the chart, and ask students to write an appropriate comparison.
   Have students at their desks also write comparisons, and have them act as editors to the board writers.
   After a number of combinations have been called out, have board writers and desk writers switch places and repeat.
Comment: You may want to explain to students that sometimes in common usage, *similar to* is used virtually interchangeably with *the same as.*

A.3.13 Do you need any _____?

Count and noncount nouns.

Procedure: On the board, write the ingredients for a recipe, putting them in two columns (count and noncount nouns) as shown below:

Stew

beef roast	water
carrots	salt
onions	pepper
potatoes	

Then ask whether any student can tell you what the grammatical difference is between the items in the first and second columns.

Explain to students that count nouns can usually be made plural by adding -*s,* but noncount nouns normally do not appear in the plural. Next, write a short sample dialogue on the board:

T: Anselmo, I want you to make stew. Will you need *any* water?
A: Yes, I'll need *some* water.
T: Will you need *some* rice?
A: No, I won't need *any.*
T: Will you need *any* carrots?
A: Yes, I'll need *some.*

Ask whether any student can tell from the dialogue what the rules are for *some* and *any.* If no one can, help students analyze the dialogue to formulate the rules as follows: Use *some* or *any* in a question. Use *some* in a positive statement. In general, *any* in a negative statement. There is an exception to this rule: If the noun is a singular count noun, use *a* or *an,* as in "I don't have *an* orange." You may not wish to present this exception at this time.

Next, ask students to suggest other recipes, and to tell you their ingredients and in which column to write the ingredients.

Put one or more other recipes on the board:

Pizza

pizza crust	tomato sauce
onions	garlic
mushrooms	cheese
green peppers	

Follow-up: Divide your class into pairs, and have students take turns questioning each other about whether they need specific ingredients for the different recipes written on the board.

Circulate, listening for errors. When you hear a lot of correct questions and answers, erase the model dialogue and have students continue their dialogues from memory.

Comment: You may need to have students brainstorm a list of ingredients that do *not* appear in the recipes and write them on the board in order to help them easily elicit the negative responses.

Variation: Have one member of each pair take turns asking the other what he or she had for dinner the night before (e.g., "Did you eat any noodles?") or what is in his or her wallet ("Do you have any stamps?").

A.3.14   Where's it at?

Prepositions of place.

Procedure: If you are presenting prepositions of place for the first time, give just a few to begin. Therefore, you could initially draw just the table, the vase, the cat, and the flowers that are part of the following illustration:

105

Language-based activities

Begin by pointing to each object and stating where it is, stressing the pronunciation of the prepositions; for example, the vase is *on* the table, the flowers are *in* the vase, the cat is *under* the table. You may also want to write the prepositions on the drawing as you present them.

Once students have had time to process these prepositions, erase them and point to the objects, asking the students to tell you where they are in relationship to other objects: T: "Where's the cat?" S: "The cat is *under* the table."

Next, add the chair and pictures to your illustration and repeat the procedure.

Still later, add the figures at the door.

Variations:

1. Send a student to the board, tell him or her a preposition, and have him or her point to the object it applies to.
2. Have the student point to other objects and tell you the prepositions that apply.
3. Have a "picture dictation": Have a student dictate a sentence that contains a preposition (e.g., "There's a lion in the corner.)" Illustrate the sentence on the board, or have other students draw it; or dictate a sentence and have students draw it.

A.3.15 Adding on

Reviewing grammatical rules through examples.

Procedure: Begin by writing on the board a list of two or three items that share a grammatical feature.

Example:

Geographical names – countries and people:

Asia – Asians	China – Chinese
America – Americans	Taiwan – Taiwanese
Egypt – Egyptians	Sudan – Sudanese

Then challenge students to come up with as many additional items as they can and add them or have a student add them to the list.

Additional examples:

Geographical names *with* the:	*Geographical names* *without* the:
the Alps	(Mount) Everest
the Atlantic Ocean	Lake Victoria
the United States	Turkey

Nouns with irregular plurals	*Verbs with irregular third persons*
gentleman – gentlemen	have – has
knife – knives	do – does
goose – geese	go – goes

Comparatives	*Irregular comparatives*
with more	*and superlatives*
challenge – more challenging	bad – worse – worst
reliable – more reliable	good – better – best

Verbs with irregular	*Modals*
past tense forms	can
spin – spun	will
shake – shook	would
creep – crept	

Two- and three-word
phrasal verbs
stand up
stand up to
stand for

Follow-up: Have students use the listed words in sentences.
Acknowledgment: This activity is based on one in Adrian Doff, *Teach English: A Training Course for Teachers* (1988).

A.3.16 Participial adjectives

Clarifying the common difference in usage of participial adjectives ending in *-ing* and those ending in *-ed*.

Procedure: Use a drawing such as the one shown on the next page to illustrate that *usually* the *-ed* form of a participial adjective applies to what we feel internally and that the *-ing* form *usually* applies to something external that causes this feeling.

Have students dictate sentences for you to write on the board that use the participial adjectives you have presented in your illustrated example.
Examples:

The flowers are pleasing.	I am pleased by the flowers.
This book is interesting.	Khoa is interested in his book.
That TV program is boring.	I'm bored with that TV program.
A bad storm can be frightening.	Alice is frightened by bad storms.

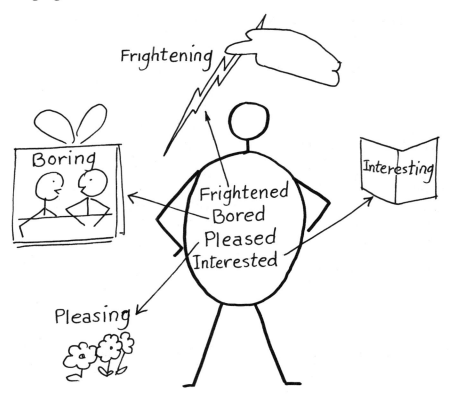

Follow-up: Have students, in class or as homework, construct their own examples of sentences using other participial adjectives such as *confusing* and *confused, depressing* and *depressed, annoying* and *annoyed, exciting* and *excited.*

Have several students write their sentences on the board and (optional) illustrate them.

Work with the class to correct any grammatical errors.

A.3.17 Ordering adjectives

Preparation: Find an object that possesses a number of qualities that can be described with adjectives. A piece of clothing, especially one that is plaid, striped, or checked, works well.

Procedure: Hold up the object you have chosen. For example, hold up a colorful pair of bathing trunks so that all members of the class can see it, and then pass it around for closer inspection.

When you have the object in hand again, ask a student, "What is this?" Permit the student to confer with others if necessary.

When the correct answer has been given, write it on the board.

Continue to ask relevant questions randomly such as, "What is it made of?" "What color(s) is it?" "What size?" "Where was it made?" "Is it new or old?" "What shape is it?" "Is it beautiful or ugly?" "Is it expensive or cheap?" "What else can you say about it?"

Write the answers randomly on the board as you receive them. Label each answer as shown in the following examples.

Examples:

trunks (noun)
cotton (material)
purple and green striped (color/pattern)
large (size)
made in America or American-made (origin)
new (age)
outrageous (observation or opinion)
men wear them or men's (qualifier)
a pair (determiners)
bathing (qualifier)

Then write: This is a _____ trunks.

Tell the students to organize the information and change its form if needed in order to fill in the blank so that the sentence they create uses all the information and orders it correctly.

You can then proceed in one of several ways:

1. You might ask all the students to work individually at their desks; then have the student who comes closest to being correct write his or her sentence on the board so that the whole class can work on correcting it.
2. You might have students take turns at the board, inserting the information where they believe it should go (but do not allow any incorrect placements to stand).

When the information has been ordered correctly, help students formulate the rule for ordering adjectives: *determiner(s) + observation or opinion + physical description: size, shape, age, color + origin + material + qualifier(s) + noun* by labeling each type of information they have used.

Finally, hold up the object again and ask the class or a student, "What is this?"

Gradually erase the ordered adjectives and keep asking, "What is this?" until all adjectives are erased and the students are responding entirely from memory: *This is a pair of outrageous, large, new, purple and green striped, American-made, cotton, men's bathing trunks.*

Follow-up: Bring the object to subsequent classes in order to practice.

Variations: Other objects you might use are *a lovely, long, rectangular, old, navy blue with white dots, made-in-Taiwan, silk, ladies' neck scarf;* or *a pair of ordinary, one-size-fits-all, new, black, wool and nylon, men's dress socks.*

Acknowledgment: I learned this activity from colleagues in the 1993 summer ESL program at the University of New Hampshire.

A.3.18 Ordering sentences: Frequency, place, and time

Procedure: Write across the top of a substantial amount of board space the most common order for constructing a simple, declarative sentence in English that contains expressions of frequency, place, and time. Underneath, write some sample sentences:

Subject	Frequency	Verb	Direct object	Place + Time	
Noun	*Adverb*		*Noun*	*Prepositional phrases*	
Americans	often	eat	dinner	in a restaurant	on Saturday night
Students	rarely	study			on Saturday night

Ask students to brainstorm words and phrases and list them under each of the word order categories.

Have students compose sentences by combining one entry from each category; then circulate, looking over students' shoulders, and select examples for students to write on the board.

When students have successfully demonstrated their ability to form these kinds of sentences, explain and demonstrate that expressions of frequency, place, and/or time can also appear at the beginning of a sentence; for example, "Frequently in the United States on Saturday night, people eat dinner in a restaurant."

Follow-up: Ask students to write sentences about what they themselves always (or sometimes, usually, seldom, never) do and define where, when, and/or how they do it; for example, I always wanted to ride a horse on a beach in the moonlight." Or ask them to write negative sentences about what they don't usually (often, never) do; for example, "I never watch wrestling matches on TV."

Acknowledgment: This activity is based on one in Elaine Kirn, *Scenario 1: English Grammar in Context* (1984).

A.3.19 Unscrambling sentences

Reviewing syntax and reminding students of articles and prepositions.

Procedure: Write scrambled sentences on the board; then have the first student to find the correct solution write it on the board.

Example for low-intermediate students: the the ate fish cat

Example for high-intermediate to advanced students: in to sat window wash the itself cat the

Follow-up: Have students write sentences and scramble them to challenge their peers. Check these sentences before their authors put them on the board so as not to frustrate students by having them work on an erroneous sentence.

Comment: To be sure that you write the correct words on the board, write the sentence on paper first and copy the words onto the board, ticking off the words as you put them on the board so as not to omit or duplicate any.

Or, if you want to use a sentence directly out of your head, take the words in their normal order but write them in different places randomly all over the board so that they become scrambled.

This is a good activity to use to wind down at the end of a class or while you wait for late arrivals. Or use it when you are doing group work and one group finishes early.

A.3.20 Sentence substitution

Exploring the various ways of expressing an idea in English.

Procedure: Write a sentence on the board – from your course book or one you've made up – that contains adjectives and adverbs.

Ask students to change one or two words at a time while keeping the sentence about the same length as the original. If necessary, allow them to change the meaning; the end result, however, should make sense and be grammatically correct.

Invite students to go to the board to make substitutions; or to save time, have them tell you or a scribe what to erase and what to add.

A.3.21 Sentence development

Working with word forms, grammatical constructions, and syntax.

Procedure: Write a simple sentence on the board, leaving ample space between words so that additional words (such as adjectives and adverbs), phrases, and clauses can be inserted.

Example

The   boy   played   a   tune   on his   violin.

Next, invite students to enrich this sentence by adding:

- Adjective(s) to describe the boy.
- Adverb(s) to describe how he played.
- Adjective(s) to describe the tune.
- Adjective(s) to describe his violin.

Using a different color of chalk or marker, write in each addition as students suggest it, or have a scribe do this, and ask the class whether the addition is grammatically correct and may remain, or is incorrect and must be erased.

Once completed, the embellished sentence might look something like this:

The *young* boy *softly* played a *happy* tune on his *beautiful new* violin.

If your students are not yet working at an intermediate level or above, you may want to stop here. If they are more advanced, ask them to add:

- An introductory adverb clause.
- A restrictive or nonrestrictive clause to describe the boy or something belonging to him (e.g., his talent, a member of his family, his name, his looks, or personality).
- An independent clause.

The embellished sentence then might look something like this:

Because he was trying not to disturb his mother, the *young* boy, *whose name was Eric, softly* played a *happy* tune on his *beautiful new* violin; *but his mother heard him anyway.*

A.3.22 Sentence reduction

Reducing long sentences to their essential elements to help in the understanding of grammatical structures.

Procedure: Choose a long sentence from your course book, or make one up and write it on the board.

Example: When I was in the train station in Amsterdam, a man who appeared to be an employee there and who wanted to help me store my luggage in a locker was actually a thief and well known to the station police; so when they saw him talking to me, they chased him away and probably saved me from some kind of mischief or worse.

Then ask students to delete from one to three words at a time. They must end up with a short but complete and grammatical sentence that is meaningful but doesn't have to mean the same as the original.

Using a different color of chalk or marker from the one used for the sentence, put parentheses around the suggested deletions, (e.g., *in a locker*).

Then ask the class to determine whether what is left is correct. If it is, erase the words in parentheses.

Reduced in this manner, the sentence above could become: *The man was known.*

Comment: Allow minor changes in word form, punctuation, or word order if necessary.

A.3.23 Grammar ticktacktoe

Constructing sentences using grammar items to be practiced.

Procedure: Draw a ticktacktoe grid on the blackboard that contains, for example, the infinitive form of verbs that have irregular past tense forms:

to put	to see	to make
to go	to do	to think
to be	to take	to sink

Next, divide your class into two teams.

Team A composes a sentence using one of the verbs in the past tense.

Team B decides whether the sentence is correct, and you decide whether team B's assessment is right or wrong.

Variations: Instead of using irregular verbs, use adverbs of frequency (i.e., *seldom, always, never, often, occasionally, sometimes, frequently, rarely,* and *usually*), phrasal verbs, or modals.

A.4 Writing

This section contains a number of *sets* of activities. Before students begin to write academic papers, for example, you might want to introduce them to the writing process, the linear structure of English, and outlining (see Activities A.4.10, A.4.11, and A.4.12). Activities A.4.13, A.4.14, and A.4.15 will help with the actual writing of their academic papers. (Note, too, that Activity A.5.6 – to be found in the Reading Comprehension section – will help students become familiar with the meanings of some common academic abbreviations they may need to use in their own writing.) Finally, Activities A.4.18, A.4.19, and A.4.20 will help them prepare for correction and revision.

If students are writing letters, on the other hand, Activities A.4.9 and A.4.17 are designed to help.

Writing pattern poems is the subject of yet another set of activities (Activities A.4.6, A.4.7, and A.4.8) that provide grammar practice as well as experience in writing in a way that is perhaps new, liberating, and fun.

A.4.1 Capitalization
A.4.2 Punctuation
A.4.3 She says/he says
A.4.4 What happens next?
A.4.5 Telling and writing a story
A.4.6 Writing a list poem
A.4.7 Sense or nonsense
A.4.8 Writing a grammar poem
A.4.9 Composing class letters
A.4.10 The writing process: Narrowing topics, finding subtopics, and organizing information
A.4.11 A train of thought: Presenting the linear structure of English written discourse
A.4.12 Constructing outlines
A.4.13 Basic formatting of academic (nonresearch) papers
A.4.14 Preparing for research paper writing
A.4.15 Paraphrasing
A.4.16 Citing sources in research papers
A.4.17 Basic formatting of business letters
A.4.18 Symbols and abbreviations used in marking student errors

Language-based activities

A.4.19   Checking for correct and varied sentence construction
A.4.20   Improving writing style

See also:

A.5.1   From A to Z
A.5.3   Read, illustrate, and retell (paraphrasing)
A.5.5   Organizational markers and meaning
A.5.6   Abbreviations: Common and academic
A.6.1   Write the numbers
A.6.3   Writing, illustrating, and performing dialogues and skits
A.7.4   What I learned from today's class; questions I have about today's material (summarizing, using concrete examples)
B.2.5   Setting class, team, pair, or individual agendas (a writing agenda)
B.2.7   Presenting a large-scale project (a newsletter)
B.3.4   A message in a bottle

A.4.1 Capitalization

Preparation: Select or compose a series of phrases or sentences containing a number of different examples of the use of capitalization.
Examples:

in London, England
the month of May
on Pleasant Street
the World Health Organization
the Stop & Shop grocery store
Pedro's wife, Ida
Juana is from Mexico.
We went to Chicago, Illinois, last June.
Why was Tim absent on Tuesday?
Have you read the novel *Moby Dick?*
May I help you?
Carlotta was married in August.
Have you been to Rockefeller Center in New York City?
Arturo was born in Spain but lives in Switzerland and speaks Spanish and French.
Is the new Walmart store located on Amherst Street or Amherst Road?

Procedure: Write your prepared phrases or sentences on the board.

Ask students to find examples within the sentences or phrases in which similar words are capitalized and to formulate rules to cover those situations.

If your students are literate in a first language that uses the roman alphabet, ask them to compare the rules of capitalization that apply in English to the rules in their first language and to make a list of the rules that are different in English.

Follow-ups:

1. Erase the prepared examples and, later in the class or at the next class, write the same examples on the board but do not capitalize any letters.

   Have students go to the board and have them apply, in one of the following ways, the rules of capitalization they have learned. If your students are of elementary school age or if they are just learning the roman alphabet, have them erase lowercase letters and replace them with capital letters as needed. If your students do not need practice writing capital letters in English, you may want them to merely circle or underline the letters to be capitalized, using chalk or a marker in a color different from the one you used.
2. Select or write different examples, and follow the procedure above.

117

3. For homework, tell your students to look at an English language newspaper or other source written in English, copy out at least three phrases or sentences that contain capitalization, bring the examples to class, and be prepared to write them on the board and explain why the capital letters are used.

A.4.2 Punctuation

Common marks of punctuation, their names, and their uses.

Procedure: Challenge students to draw on the board and label as many marks of punctuation as they can recall. Each student should produce at least one mark. A group effort may be required to produce all the marks shown here.

'	apostrophe
*	asterisk
:	colon
,	comma
--	dash (or —)
. . .	ellipses
!	exclamation point
-	hyphen
(	parenthesis; ( ) parentheses
.	period
?	question mark
"	quotation marks
;	semicolon

'	single quotation mark
/	slash
[ ]	square brackets

When the list has been completed to your satisfaction, review the uses for each mark and (optional) have students write sentences illustrating the proper use of each one.

Allow time for students to copy the list into their notebooks.

A.4.3 She says/he says

Writing dialogue.

Procedure: Draw a comic strip containing stick figures interacting. Draw an empty dialogue balloon above each figure's head. The comic strip should contain as many individual scenes as you have pairs or small groups of students. If you want students to practice specific vocabulary, include items or situations in the scenes that will provide opportunities for them to do this, as shown in the example here.

119

Language-based activities

Next, assign one scene to each pair or group of students.

Have them decide what each character in their scene is saying, and have them write the dialogue in the appropriate balloon.

Finally, have students read their dialogues aloud.

Comment: Because all the pairs or groups will be writing without consulting each other, some very funny dialogue can result!

Follow-ups:

1. Have students select the scene in which they think the dialogue works best and revise the rest of the comic strip to be in harmony with that scene.
2. Use the scenes to practice grammatical constructions such as the present progressive: *is sitting, is reading, is sleeping,* and so on, by pointing to each scene or figure and asking: "What is happening?" or "What is this figure doing?"
3. Have pairs or groups of students draw comic strips and have pairs or groups compose the dialogue. Select some of the best for board display.

Additional examples:

Example 1

Example 2

Example 3

Example 4

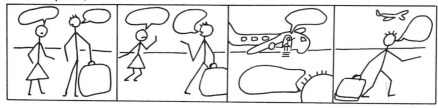

A.4.4 What happens next?

Writing a story.

Procedure: On the board, write an opener – part of a sentence or a sentence or two that begin to tell a story – and have students complete the story in three sentences or less.

Examples:

1. Tatiana's house is situated in the middle of a deep woods. It cannot be seen from the road, and the nearest neighbor's house is a mile

   away. _____

   _____ .

2. The telephone rang at 2 a.m., and _____

   _____ .

3. Jacques' ambition was to appear on a TV game show. One day last year, _____

_____ .

Assign the same opener to all the students so that they can compare similarities and differences in their outcomes.

When students have finished, have pairs help each other edit.

Then select three students or more, space permitting, to write their completions on the board.

Discuss and do further editing, if needed.

Comment: Displaying the writing publicly, and comparing it, stimulates interest, promotes discussion of both content and the writing itself, and encourages self-editing and peer editing.

A.4.5   Telling and writing a story

Procedure: Draw some figures and perhaps some objects on the board, or have students draw for you.

Example:

Draw a scene such as the one shown here.

Ask a student to tell something about the drawing in one sentence and write the sentence on the board. Also, encourage students to name the figures.

Have another student add a sentence.

When students can no longer add a new sentence, add a new figure or object or change or erase one that was originally drawn. Then ask students to add sentences to the story that reflect the new illustration. Continue making changes and challenging students to add sentences as many times as you wish.

Variation: Ask students to do the adding or erasing of an element in the illustration. Or ask them to change the time (tense) of the story.

You can also use this activity for specific grammar practice, if you choose. The present progressive ("Two men are fighting.") works well, for example.

Comment: This activity works with any level. If you have a beginning-level class, you can write the sentences on the board that the students dictate. With an intermediate level or above, have a scribe write them.

When the written story is "finished," you may want to ask the students to review the story so that they can make whatever improvements they can, for example, add connectors and transitions, combine sentences, or delete unnecessary repetition.

Of course, if you have limited time or a large class, you can simply draw the illustrations and have the students respond orally.

More examples:

A.4.6 Writing a list poem

Procedure: To illustrate to the students what kind of writing they will do, choose a topic such as:

- An upcoming holiday
- Their native country
- Horses
- Envy

- Parts of the body
- Things we remember
- School

Once the topic is chosen, have students brainstorm, telling you everything that comes to mind when they think of the topic. Take *envy* as an example; write their words, phrases, or sentences on the board:

Envy

green with envy: jealousy   green emeralds   toads   hurting
longing: can't have something someone else has
wanting: envious of friends, money, position, fame
cars: expensive cars: Jags   Porsches   BMWs

Choose some of these student contributions and begin setting them out in lines:

Can't have something someone else has
Can't be somebody else

Then begin to ask questions: "What can't you have?" "Who can't you be?" Again write down students' responses:

Can't have expensive dogs, jewels
Can't be famous movie stars

Then ask students to select some of the answers and begin to organize them into lines. In this activity, you are not only the scribe but also an editor, an active participant, and you, too, can contribute suggestions, make selections, and choose to ignore brainstorm material that doesn't work.

Once a rough first draft is complete, try experimenting, moving lines around, and adding details. Prompt students to try to find more expressive nouns and more active verbs. Look for ways to create surprises, drama, and comedy. Point out pleasing sound combinations and patterns.

Thus, the "list poem" in the example above might end up looking something like this:

Envy

Can't be famous like Madonna and Bruce Willis
Can't drive a purple Porsche, a red Rolls
not even a green Geo
Can't parade a pair of poodles on an emerald leash
Can't live forever
like Elvis and Lassie

Finally, help students edit for grammar, spelling, and mechanics.

Follow-up: Have students work on creating list poems in small groups or pairs or individually.

Let them choose their own topics. Give them sufficient time, allowing them to continue their work in a subsequent class or as homework, if necessary.

Have them write their finished poems on the board to share with the whole class.

Variation: You can use this activity to practice grammatical structures. Instead of a topic, give them a structure to use, such as *I wish I were . . . / . . . could . . . / . . . had . . .; If I were . . . , / I would . . .;* or *I always . . . / I seldom . . . / I never. . . .*

Acknowledgment: This activity is based on Larry Fagin, *The List Poem: A Guide to Teaching & Writing Catalog Verse* (1991).

A.4.7   Sense or nonsense

Writing a poem; practicing word forms (nouns and verbs).

Procedure: Divide your class into two groups.

Ask one group to come up with the names of ten things (nouns). These items can all relate to a common idea or theme chosen by the group, or not be related at all. Let the students decide.

Ask the second group to come up with ten verbs.

Keep the two groups sufficiently separate so that neither knows what the other is writing.

Once the groups have settled on their words, have a scribe from each group write the lists on the board.

Then the first group sends a writer to the board to write a line of a poem using one noun and one verb from the lists. Members of the board writer's group can help the writer with ideas, grammar, spelling, and so on. When the line is finished, the writer erases or strikes through the noun and the verb from the lists so they cannot be used again.

Example:

turtle	marry
~~engine~~	~~wait~~
~~moon~~	hurry
jelly	kiss
school	~~leave~~
juice	arrive
~~fish~~	fall
silverware	touch
map	fix
mountain	~~break~~

The moon breaks from behind a cloud
As fish leave their hiding places
An engine waits to be started
. . .

When a group finishes a line, members of the other group can correct any errors, or corrections can be done by the whole class or by you at the end of the activity. (You may need to set a time limit for each writer at the board.) Groups alternate until there are no more nouns and verbs left to use.

Variations: Require that all verbs be in the past tense or another tense, or that they all be transitive or passive, or that the sentences all be declarative or interrogative or complex.

Comment: Expect grammaticality but not necessarily literal "sense." When students are not limited to expressing themselves literally, the experience can be liberating: They can concentrate more on form, and it can be great fun.

Then, if a student writes a line such as "the mountain kisses the sky," encourage discussion of *how* the line is "true" and therefore "makes sense."

A.4.8 Writing a grammar poem

Using predetermined parts of speech (word forms) to compose a five-line poem.

Procedure: Write the following rules on the board and tell students they're to write a poem using them:

Line 1 consists of just one noun.
Line 2 consists of two adjectives, joined by *and,* that describe the noun.
Line 3 consists of a verb and an adverb that tell what the noun is doing and how it is doing it.
Line 4 is a simile; that is, it begins with *like* or *as* and is followed by a comparison.
Line 5 is in question form.

You may want to begin by providing a model of the poem on the board before students write.
Example:

> Comprehension
> difficult and necessary
> waiting impatiently
> like a door to be opened
> where can I find the key?

Or, you may want to begin with the whole class dictating suggestions for you to use in constructing an original model on the board.

When students have a model, have them write poems following the rules.

Encourage them to search for synonyms (a thesaurus is useful) and to try alternative images – to revise and refine.

Select some of the poems to be displayed on the board.

Variation(s):

1. Follow the procedure above, except change the rule for the last line to read: Line 5 is in the conditional; it begins with *if only* and expresses a wish (e.g., *if only I could find the key*).
2. Choose a theme or a new vocabulary word so that all students start with something in common. See where the poems go from there, and have some students write theirs on the board.

127

A.4.9 Composing class letters

Presenting letter writing and social conventions for thank-you letters, requests, and invitations.

Preparation: Watch for opportunities for your class to write letters in English such as a letter to a sick classmate, a thank-you to a staff person for special help, a request to a school official for a special piece of equipment or for a special privilege, or an invitation to an interesting member of the community to visit your classroom and speak to your class.

If your students are learning English in an English-speaking country or writing to a native speaker of English, this activity will begin to make them aware of the need to learn the social conventions of the new culture as well as its letter-writing conventions.

If all your students come from a culture that has very different social conventions with regard to these kinds of letters, you may need to present some models to discuss with your class in advance.

Procedure: Explain to your students the reason for writing the letter. Tell them that this will be a class project and that the letter you will send will be composed of parts of different students' individual letters.

Ask students to brainstorm and to make a list of important information that the letter should contain. Write their ideas on the board as they contribute them.

Then ask the students to decide what information should come first, second, and so on.

Finally, ask as many students as possible to begin to compose their letters on the board, keeping a portion of board free. Use this free space for transcription of the composite letter.

As students write at the board, circle or otherwise call attention to phrases, sentences, or larger pieces of writing that might be appropriate for your composite letter. You may have to issue broad hints in order to get students to provide everything you will need for a good composite letter. If more than one student's writing contains a possible selection for the composite, ask students to help you choose which one to use.

Be sure to involve students who are writing at their desks as editors. Read over their shoulders and consider their writing for contributions to the letter.

As parts of the letter are selected for inclusion in the composite, copy them onto the open area of the board.

Continue until all aspects of the letter – from date and salutation to closing – have been provided by the students.

You will probably have to do some editing to ensure that all the composite parts of the letter cohere.

Ask a student who has legible handwriting to copy the letter onto appropriate stationery and circulate it for everyone to sign.

A.4.10 The writing process: Narrowing topics, finding subtopics, and organizing information

Procedure: To demonstrate how to narrow a topic or to find subtopics that can be used to develop an idea or a thesis, show students how to use *listing* or *clustering*. Then show students how to use *columns* to help organize and develop their topic as well as produce an outline of their paper.

On the board write several general subjects about which students would be likely to have some knowledge and in which they might have some interest, for example, computers, American music, soccer mania, the AIDS epidemic.

Ask them to choose one of the subjects; erase the others.

Then have students tell you what comes to mind when they think of this subject, and list the results of their brainstorming on the board:

Example:

LISTING

Computers
PCs
e-mail
text editing
the Internet
computerized banking

Explain that each entry on this list now represents a subtopic that can be used to develop a paper on computers or that each one can be considered in and of itself as a possible topic for a paper. If the subtopics are still too large, choose one and repeat the brainstorming process:

The Internet
search engines
Web pages
evaluating Internet resources
the Internet as a commercial outlet
historical development of the Internet
hackers

129

Language-based activities

CLUSTERING

Follow the procedure above, but write the subject students have selected in the middle of the board and circle it. Then, instead of listing the students' brainstorming ideas, write them in a "web" around the subject. Indicate relationships by drawing connecting lines:

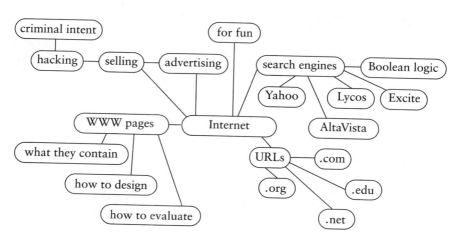

COLUMNS

Show students graphically how to organize and develop their topic and how to compose an outline of their paper by placing their subtopics in columns:

Using Internet search engines

Paragraph topic	*Supporting details*
Some popular search engines	1. Yahoo
	2. Lycos
	3. AltaVista
How to use them:	1. Boolean logic
	2. Other

Comment: Make students aware that these processes will help them not only to narrow subjects into workable paper topics but also to develop topics for oral presentations and, in addition, that they can apply these processes when they need to write answers to essay questions on tests.

A.4.11 A train of thought: The linear structure of English written discourse

Procedure: To illustrate the linear nature of academic or argument-based writing in English, I use the concept suggested by the idiom *train of thought,* as in the frequently heard expression "I've lost my train of thought."

I draw a train's engine on the board to represent the introduction to a piece of writing. I tell students that, just as the train's destination is known by the engineer and perhaps displayed on the outside of the engine, the introduction should tell the reader explicitly where the writing is headed by displaying a topic or thesis statement.

The cars attached to the engine represent the paragraphs that support and develop the topic or thesis.

The caboose is, of course, the conclusion.

The couplings that connect the parts of the train represent transitions and other types of connectors that link sentence to sentence and paragraph to paragraph.

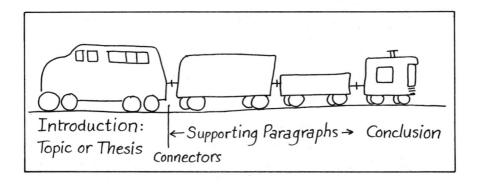

Introduction: Topic or Thesis ←Supporting Paragraphs→ Conclusion Connectors

I explain that writers of English, perhaps Americans in particular, usually want to get directly to the point of a piece of writing, just as a train needs to get to its destination quickly and without unnecessary detours even if an attractive diversion presents itself along the way.

Comment: Be sure that your students understand that (1) different cultures may organize ideas and communication differently and (2) if they know what the difference is between their culture's organization and that of English speakers, they will be better able to understand English and will be more effective at organizing their own communication in English so that other English speakers will be more likely to understand them. Be sure that they also understand that (3) although linear structure is important (since it is internationally accepted when communicating in English), this does not mean that one culture's system is better than another, only that it is different.

A.4.12 Constructing outlines

Preparation: Choose a paragraph or short essay from your course book or other source for students to use to practice outlining.

Procedure: To present the concept of outlining, write the following on the board:

I.
II. A.
   B.
      1.
      2.
         a.
         b.

This illustration can be used to explain to students that if there is a *I*, there must be a *II*; if an *A*, a *B*; and so on.

Erase *a.* and *b.* to show that subdivisions are not used unless they are required by the subject matter that is being outlined.

Add *3.* under the *b.* to show that as many subdivisions as needed may be included.

Add *III.* to show that as many major divisions as needed may be included.

Erase your illustration.

Give students your preselected reading material, and ask them to outline it.

Circulate among students working at their desks and select one student to write an outline of the material on the board for discussion and for editing, if needed. Or have two students present alternative outlines on the board for comparison and discussion.

Follow-up: At the next class, ask for a volunteer to present a review of the rules of outlining, using the board to illustrate.

A.4.13 Basic formatting of academic (nonresearch) papers

Procedure: Using a large segment of board, draw an outline that represents the first page of an academic writing assignment and on which you can illustrate the format students should use when preparing an academic paper. The example shown here follows the rules outlined by the *MLA Handbook for Writers of Research Papers,* the style sheet I teach and one that is widely used:

Example:

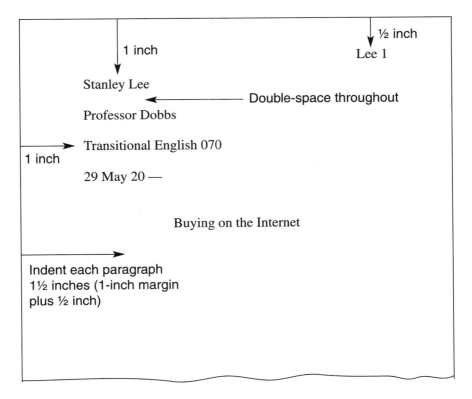

- Use 1-inch margins on all sides.
- The student's full name, teacher's name, course name and number, and date are placed on separate lines in the upper left side of the first page; the student's last name and the page number are placed in the top right corner of the first page and each subsequent page.
- The title is centered on the first page (under the name and other material); the first letter of the first and last word are capitalized, and

the first letter of all words in between are capitalized except articles and prepositions.

- The text is double-spaced.
- Each new paragraph is indented ½ inch.

Because students may lack the necessary vocabulary to understand your directions, you may want to label your illustration with technical words you use such as *margin, indent,* and *double-space.*

For additional information to provide to students on the formatting of research papers such as quoting directly, using in-line citation, and attaching a Works Cited page (Bibliography), see Activity A.4.16.

Comment: Presenting this information step-by-step on the board or on an overhead transparency gives students opportunities to question each item in turn as well as time to absorb each instruction before new information is added; and it duplicates the actual, manual process of formatting a research paper. I therefore prefer this method instead of giving students a handout or sending them to a printed source.

Allow time for students to copy the information into their notebooks.

A.4.14 Preparing for research paper writing

Practicing note taking; learning how to avoid plagiarism by employing a different format for note cards containing (1) direct quotations, (2) paraphrases, or (3) personal observations about original material.

Procedure: Draw three representations of a 3 × 5 inch note card on the board. On them show students how to record information from a text.

Direct quotation:

Name	Author's last name.
".............................	Author's exact words in
....	quotation marks.
.............................." (26)	Page number in parentheses.

Paraphrase:

Name

....   Same meaning as author's

....   but using your own words

.... (26)   and word order.

Personal observations about the material you have read:

Name, work, page number

[................? ....   Questions or observations

....   about the work in square

.................................]   brackets so that you'll recall

they're your ideas, not the

author's.

Next, have students practice research paper note taking. Select a page from your course book – perhaps from a recent assignment – so that all students are working on the same basic material. Have students:

1. Record a direct quotation.
2. Write a paraphrase of a sentence or short passage.
3. Write a personal comment about what they have read.

Ask for volunteers or choose students to write one of their practice "cards" on the board for discussion and for editing, if needed.

A.4.15 Paraphrasing

Preparation: Select a sentence from a text in your course book or from some other relevant reading material. A topic sentence or a sentence containing specific details works well.

Procedure: Write the sentence at the top of the board. Give a brief, general explanation of the process of paraphrasing. Then:

1. Ask students to talk about what the writer means.

   Listen for synonyms of key words; write them on the board. If you don't hear any, ask students to find and underline the key words in the sentence.

   Ask for synonyms of the underlined words and write them on the board. Try to obtain several synonyms for each key word. Discuss with the students the relative merits of the various synonyms; circle or underline those that seem most appropriate.

   Point out words that lack good synonyms and must be used directly, without paraphrase.

2. Ask students to write a sentence paraphrasing the original, using the synonyms they prefer.

   Circulate, looking over shoulders, and find three or more sentences using different synonyms.

   Ask the writers to put these sentences on the board next to the original.

3. Ask students to work again with the original sentence, rearranging its word order to form a sentence with different syntax but being careful not to change the meaning of the original.

   Choose examples for the board. Add your own examples, if needed.

4. Have students change the word order of the sentence they wrote using synonyms (in step 2) without changing meaning.

   Again, select students to put examples on the board.

   Discuss the strengths and weaknesses of each example.

5. Show students how to cite the source (see Activity A.4.16).

Follow-up: Using different sentences, repeat the process as needed. Or repeat it using a short paragraph.

A.4.16 Citing sources in research papers

Quoting directly, using in-line citations, preparing a Works Cited page.

Preparation: Students should be familiar with the basic formatting of nonresearch, academic papers (see Activity A.4.13).

Procedure for quoting directly: Draw an outline representing a page of a research paper on a large segment of board and illustrate the format described here that students should use when quoting directly. The examples in the activity follow the rules outlined in the *MLA Handbook for Writers of Research Papers,* the style sheet I teach and one which is widely used:

1. When quoting prose directly, put the quoted words in quotation marks unless the quotation is more than four typed lines.
2. When quoting prose that is more than four lines in length, use no quotation marks, but "double-indent"; that is, indent 1 inch.
3. When quoting poetry directly, put the quoted words in quotation marks unless the quotation is more than three typed lines.
4. When quoting poetry that is more than three typed lines, use no quotation marks, but double-indent; that is, indent 1 inch.
5. To show an omission in a direct quotation, use an ellipsis (three dots: spaced) for example, . . . ; if the ellipsis comes at the end of a sentence, add a period, for example, ...
6. To show that something has been changed or added to a direct quotation, put the changed or added material in square brackets, for example, [added information].

Procedure for using in-line citations: Using the illustration of a direct quotation you have just written on the board, add the following use of in-line citations:

7. Unless an author's name is mentioned in the text, put the author's last name or, if the name is unknown, a shortened title, in parentheses along with the page number where the original quotation can be found: (a) If the in-line citation is being used after a direct quotation of four or fewer lines of prose or of three or fewer lines of poetry, or following a paraphrase or following your own comments, put a period after the end parentheses, for example, (Name 22). But (b) if the in-line citation is being used after an extended quotation of more than four lines that does not need quotation marks because of its indented format, put the period at the end of the quotation and the citation after the period, for example, (Name 22)

Language-based activities

Example for items 1 and 7a:

> "put the quoted words in quotation marks unless the quotation is more than four typed lines" and put the period after the citation (Name 22).

Example for items 2, 3, and 7b:

> When quoting prose that runs over four typed lines or poetry that runs over three typed lines, use no quotation marks; instead, double-indent: that is, indent 1 inch and put the period before the citation. (Name 22)

Procedure for attaching a Works Cited page (Bibliography): Using a large segment of board, draw another outline representing a Works Cited page on which you can illustrate the format students should follow to acknowledge the sources they have used in their research paper writing:

- Title the page *Works Cited,* and center the title.
- Order the list of works alphabetically.
- Cite the author's last name first, followed by the first name and middle name or initial, if given; if author is unknown, cite the title of the work first.
- Begin the first line of the first entry at the left margin.
- Indent the second and all subsequent lines of each entry ½ inch.
- Double-space all entries.
- Use italics or underlining for the titles of books, magazines, journals, newspapers, plays, films, databases.
- Put the titles of articles and short stories – pieces of writing that are part of a larger whole – in quotation marks.

See illustration on the next page.

Comment: Because the rules for citing works on a Works Cited page are very long and complex, I find it best to illustrate only a few rules, such as those listed above, when I present the formatting of the Works Cited page on the board. I then have students use their course book as an example of a work to be cited, and together we work out an example of how it would be listed on a Works Cited page.

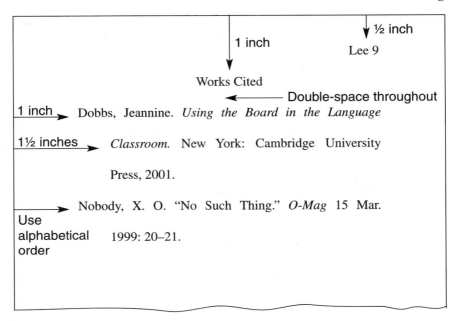

When they write their research papers, they consult the *MLA Handbook for Writers of Research Papers* to find more detailed instructions about what information to include and how to order it depending on the type of research sources they use.

A.4.17   Basic formatting of business letters

Procedure: Using a large segment of board, draw an outline representing an 8½ × 11 inch (A4) sheet of paper on which to illustrate the generally accepted format for business letters written in English. Indicate on the drawing that correct usage requires:

- For a long letter, 1-inch side margins; for a short letter, 1½-inch side margins.
- Double-spacing between paragraphs and between each element (e.g., the return address and the inside address – see example on the next page); single-spacing elsewhere.

Because students may lack the necessary vocabulary to understand your directions, you may want to label your illustration with the technical words you use such as *margin, indent,* and *single-space.* Students will, of course, also need to become familiar with the names of each of the elements of a business letter such as *return address,* and *inside address* as well as with the necessary abbreviations.

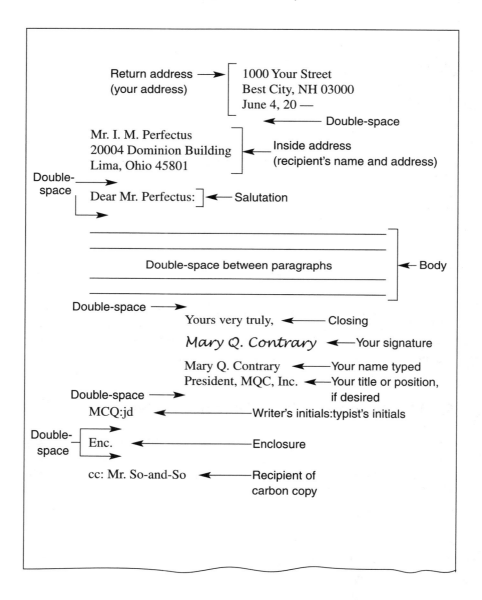

Comment: The same technique can be used to present other, more detailed aspects of letter formatting such as the differences between block (used above), full block, and semiblock as well as the formatting of envelopes.

Follow-ups:

1. To give students practice with formatting business letters, draw a mock-up of a letter on the board, using horizontal lines to represent its various elements.

   Call on students to go to the board to fill in an example of what should appear on a specific line or in a specific element.

2. Scatter words, abbreviations, and symbols, such as the ones shown here, randomly over an expanse of board and have students at their seats write them on a piece of paper in the places where they should appear.

Example of follow-up 2:

cc:	Recipient's Name	Return address	Ms.
:	,	*Your Signature, written*	
very	Dear	YN:dd	
Date		Yours	Enc.
Your Signature, typed	truly		Inside address

Note that by including the two, separate, decontextualized marks of punctuation (i.e., the colon and the comma), you will sharpen students' awareness that these marks have fixed, required, end positions, that is, after the salutation and the closing, respectively.

Next, to verify how accurate students' desk work has been:

- Have some students write their results on the board for whole-class checking and, if necessary, editing.
- Or, have students tell you or a scribe what to write on each line.
- Or, divide the class into teams and have each team's scribe write on the board what their teammates dictate.

3. For homework or in class, have students compose their own letters, using their own names and addresses, to a local business they know. If the work is done in class, a local phone directory can provide addresses.

A.4.18 Symbols and abbreviations used in marking student errors

Preparing students to revise their written work.

Preparation: On the board, draw a grid similar to the example given here, and list the symbols and abbreviations you normally use to respond to student errors.

Symbol or abbreviation	Meaning	Problem
agr	agreement	Subject and verb do not agree in number.
awk	awkward	
cap	capital	Use a capital letter.
frag	fragment	Not a complete sentence; the subject or verb is missing.
∧	insert	Something more is needed here.
¶	paragraph	Begin a new paragraph here.
ro	run on	There is more than one sentence here; insert correct punctuation.
sp	spelling	
vt	verb tense	
ww	wrong word	
?		What do you mean? Or, I can't read your writing. Or, are you sure of this?

Have students copy the grid into their notebooks. Or, to save time, prepare photocopies of the grid for students.

Procedure: Discuss the symbols and abbreviations with the students, answer any questions, and tell them to review the information as homework.

At the next class, write only the symbols and abbreviations on the board, and change their order.

Ask students to tell you their meaning without referring to their copies of the grid.

Follow-up: Write a brief example of an erroneous sentence – use examples from students' own writing if possible – using one color of chalk or marker for the sentence and another color to mark the appropriate symbol or abbreviation.

Ask students to tell you what they should do to correct the error, or have a student go to the board and do it.

Here are a few examples of erroneous sentences with an appropriate editorial response:

agr	The boy often *run* away.	*ww*	The boy often runs *always*.
sp	The boy *offen* runs away.	*cap*	*t*he boy often runs away.

A.4.19 Checking for correct and varied sentence construction

Preparation: In advance of this activity, students will need to have completed a homework assignment consisting of writing a short essay, a paraphrase, or a book review – any piece of original writing that contains one or more substantial paragraphs. (In fact, I usually have students use a second or third draft of one of these assignments, a paper that has been reviewed by peers, that I have responded to, and that has been edited and revised.)

Procedure

1. Before addressing their writing, review with your students the following rules for constructing simple, compound, complex, and compound-complex sentences:

   A *simple* sentence consists of one independent clause containing a subject and a verb, either of which may be compound. (Gillian and Hillary are friends.)

   A *compound* sentence consists of two independent clauses, connected by a semicolon or by a comma and a coordinating conjunction, for example, *and, but, for, nor, or, so, yet.* (Gillian and Hillary are friends, and they work together at the fish market.)

A *complex* sentence consists of an independent clause plus a subordinate clause. (Gillian and Hillary work together at the fish market that is located on Dock Street.)

A *compound-complex* sentence consists of two or more independent clauses plus one or more subordinate clause(s). (*Example:* After they graduated, Gillian and Hillary became friends, and now they work together at the fish market on Dock Street.)

Select four students, and assign each student one of the four kinds of sentence structures to write on the board. Students at their desks can be writing one of the kinds of sentences, too.

Ask students to:

- Draw a box around any independent clauses.
- Enclose any subordinate clauses in square brackets.
- Underline the subject of any clause once, and underline the main verb twice.
- Enclose prepositional phrases in parentheses.
- Mark coordinating conjunctions with an asterisk.
- Mark subordinating words with a pound sign.
- Circle the articles.

Example:

[After *they* graduated], Gillian and Hillary became friends, and now *they* work together (at the fish market) (on Dock Street).

With the contributions of students at their seats, help those who have done the board work to correct any errors. These sentences now serve as public models for the work that follows.

2. To check for variety in sentence structure, ask students to count the total number of sentences in the piece of writing they did as homework. Then ask them to count the number of sentences that are simple, the number that are compound, and so on.

   If they have not written any sentences in one of the categories, ask them to consider whether their writing would be improved if they included a greater variety of sentence structures. Have them revise some sentences in class or as homework if they need more variety.

   Next, have them mark (in the manner illustrated in the board work) at least one example of each different type of sentence construction they have used.

   Have them exchange their work with a partner to check for errors in constructing or marking these sentences.

3. To check for variety in length, using the same piece of writing, have students count the number of words in each of their sentences to check

whether they are using sentences of varying lengths as well as of varying construction.

Have students who have composed good examples of short and long sentences write them on the board.

Be sure that students understand that variety is not the only goal, and that *appropriate* length and construction are also to be considered: Short, simple sentences can be used to emphasize important information, and longer, compound or complex sentences can be used to illustrate relationships.

Comment: This activity is worth the time it takes; however, you may need to break it into two parts: reviewing the four kinds of sentence construction and marking their component parts in one class and having students analyze and mark their own writing in another class session.

A.4.20 Improving writing style

Revising for brevity, precision, and vigor.

Preparation: Find examples of sentences that suffer from wordiness, weak or nonspecific verbs, and/or a lack of clarity.

Use examples taken from your students' writing or other sources, or write such sentences yourself.

Procedure: Write the sentences on the board.

Decide with the students what essential information is contained in each sentence and what the problem with the sentence is. You might underline the problem(s) with a different color of chalk or marker.

Then help students restate the sentence grammatically while avoiding the problem and retaining the meaning.

Examples:

- I like *to watch* movies at home, traveling and *to work* in my garden. Needs to use parallel construction: I like watching movies at home, traveling, and gardening.
- When I was sixteen *years of age,* I got my first real job. *Sixteen* means *years of age* – delete *years of age;* the clause can also be deleted: At sixteen I got my first real job.
- It took *a long time* for the first astronauts to reach the moon. Needs to clarify what *a long time* means and whether or not the time in question is the length of the trip itself or the time spent to develop the technology to make the trip. Possible revision: It took almost 103 hours for the first astronauts to travel to the moon.

145

Language-based activities

Additional examples:

- It is hard to both hold down a job and raise a child too.
- The early life of my mother was different from mine.
- I wish to express my gratitude to you for presenting me with the opportunity to meet with you last week in Chicago.
- When my friend's dog died, she was very unhappy.

Follow-ups:

1. When your students have future writing assignments, keep them on the lookout for these types of problems in their own writing by having them spend some time rereading their papers in class expressly for this purpose and making last-minute corrections before handing them in.

   Also (or as an alternative), have them read each other's papers, looking for these kinds of problems, and have them suggest changes.
2. Instead of using discrete sentences, find a longer piece of writing that exhibits these types of problems, or make one up and duplicate it for students to work on as homework or in class.

   Then select a few examples of the students' revisions to be displayed on the board for whole-class discussion, or duplicate them if they are too long for board writing.

A.5 Reading comprehension

Although short texts can be written on the board for discussion when paper copies are not available, this kind of reproduction of reading materials is usually not very practical.

There are, nevertheless, other ways in which board writing can be used in conjunction with reading activities. For example, the classic technique of writing questions about a reading on the board and then asking students to publicly write the answers can be used with almost any reading assignment. Activity A.5.4 illustrates this technique; it uses the daily paper as a source for a scavenger hunt for information. The other activities in this section provide additional ways of linking board use to reading assignments.

See also:

A.5.1 From A to Z

Procedure: Review the names of the letters of the alphabet orally, in order, with students.

Then write the alphabet but scatter the letters randomly over the board, point to the letters, and call on students or ask for volunteers to tell you what they are.

Variations:

1. Mix small letters and capital letters and proceed as above.
2. Write words scattered randomly over the board. Point to them and ask students to spell them out.
3. Send several students to the board and have the other students write at their seats. Call out letters randomly for students to write.

A.5.2 Filling out forms

Preparation: You may want to make photocopies of the generic application form shown on the next page or design one specifically for your students to use in the second step of this activity.

Procedure:

1. On the board, draw a sample registration form, application, or other kind of form that is appropriate for your students, for example, forms to fill out for a passport, insurance, a driver's license, complaints, recommendations, customs, or applications to college, a course, or a summer camp.

   Point to the form, and ask students to read aloud what information is being called for and to give answers for you or a scribe to write in the appropriate blanks.

2. Erase the information on the board, and have students write their own, personal information in each of the blanks, using a photocopy of the application. If you cannot make photocopies, have the students copy the prompts from the board to paper before they write in their answers.

Example:

```
                          Sample Application
  Name _____
  Address _____

         _____
  Phone Number _____
  Gender _____
  Date of Birth _____
  Occupation or Status _____
  Height _____
  Weight _____
  Color of Hair _____      Color of Eyes _____
```

A.5.3 Read, illustrate, and retell

Reading, illustrating, and summarizing a descriptive piece of writing.

Preparation: Select a paragraph or short story, perhaps from your course book, that contains a lot of visual detail, or use the sample text provided here.

Make copies of your chosen text for all of your students to read as homework or in class.

Procedure: If you have sufficient board space, have each student work directly on the board, drawing an illustration to accompany the piece of writing, using stick figures, if they wish, and colored chalk or markers, if available.

If your board space is limited, ask for volunteers or appoint several students to do the board work. Encourage the students who are not drawing to make suggestions and to question the students at the board about their drawings – what they represent and so on.

When the drawings are complete, have students who did not draw explain the drawings or retell the stories using only the drawings as a guide.

Sample text: Mr. and Mrs. Harris live in a large yellow house with many windows. Cecil Harris is tall, is about 40 years old, wears glasses, and has a lot of dark curly hair. LaDonna Harris is a little younger and a lot shorter; she has red curly hair.

On weekends, the Harrises put on blue jeans and old shirts and work in their garden, around which they have built a tall fence. They have

149

planted roses and sunflowers in front of the fence. The Harrises have also placed window boxes at every window, and these boxes are filled with bright green ivy.

Recently, the Harrises bought a dog and named it Sparks. Sparks is not any special kind of dog but a mixture: Her body is brown, and she has a black head and white feet. She has a long tail and big ears.

One Saturday, Cecil Harris is digging a trench and LaDonna Harris is planting lettuce and carrot seeds in it for their vegetable garden. They do not see that Sparks is following them, digging holes in the row of newly planted seeds.

Follow-up: Let your students try their hand at writing new texts to use as the basis for this activity. You may want to discuss with students the elements their piece of writing needs in order to be suitable for this use: It should be limited to one "scene" and one activity and contain a lot of concrete, visual descriptions such as colors (if you have colored chalk or markers), sizes, names, and so on.

A.5.4 Reading English-language newspapers

Scanning for specific information; reading for comprehension of ideas.

Preparation: You will need a minimum of one English-language newspaper for each pair of students in your class; the activity works best if everyone has a copy of the same day's paper.

Procedure: Divide your class into pairs.

Write a list of items on the board for students to find in their newspapers (see examples below). As soon as a pair finds an item, one member goes to the board and writes the answer along with the page number on which it was found. Students should take turns doing the board writing.

Some items will have only one possible response, but allow pairs to provide additional, different answers when possible.

Examples of items for beginning-level students to find:

1. Name of the paper
2. Name of a country
3. Name of someone in a photograph
4. An amount of money
5. A number larger than 1,000 (not money)
6. Name of an advertiser
7. A map
8. Names of two sports
9. Name of a sports player
10. A headline

Examples for intermediate-level students:

1. Name of the paper and where it is published
2. Name of a country and why it is in the news
3. Name of the section that lists deaths
4. The weather forecast
5. The paper's index: how is it ordered?
6. Names of all sports in the sports section
7. Number of births (or deaths) listed
8. A recipe: what is it for?
9. A form to fill in
10. Name of a comic strip
11. Name of a children's or action movie

Examples for advanced-level students:

1. The 5Ws (who, what, when, where, why) in a news story
2. Names of three kinds of classified ads
3. Results of an event in their favorite sport
4. Two food ads: compare some prices
5. Two programs on TV at 8 p.m.
6. Name and rating of a movie they would like to see
7. An editorial and why they do or do not agree with the point of view of the writer
8. A photo they like: recaption it
9. A graph or table
10. A job they would like to have

Variation: This activity may be done in small groups rather than in pairs, in which case each student should have his or her own copy of the paper, or one paper can be used by each small group, with its pages spread out to allow each student to scan for information to contribute to the group's work.

Follow-up: Discuss any item(s) you or the students find particularly interesting. Elicit any knowledge, opinions, or ideas they have about the subject.

A.5.5 Organizational markers and meaning

Using a text to present organizational markers and patterns of organization.

Preparation: You will need a list of organizational markers such as:

- on the other hand
- in 1995
- likewise
- first . . . second
- because . . . therefore
- first . . . then . . . next . . . finally
- similarly
- on the contrary

- however
- after that
- as a result of
- compared to
- as a consequence
- different from
- meanwhile
- due to

Procedure: Write the names of several patterns of organization across the top of the board such as comparison and contrast, process (chronology), cause and effect, argumentation.

Read one organizational marker from your prepared list and have students decide in which column or columns it should be placed.

You can do the board writing, or a scribe can do it; or assign one student to write in each column, to give more students a chance to write.

When all the markers have been placed in the columns, have students scan a reading from a course book or other text (preferably one the students have already read), looking for organizational markers. Have the students call out the markers to you or to a scribe to circle, using a different color chalk or marker from that used to write the lists. If they find markers not on your list, add them to the ones already on the board.

When the reading has been completed, have students determine its overall, primary pattern of organization and discuss any secondary patterns that may occur within it.

Comment: Be sure that students understand that (1) recognizing patterns of organization helps them understand the development and the meaning of a text and (2) using organizational markers in their own writing will help their readers in the same ways.

A.5.6 Abbreviations: Common and academic

Preparation: Select abbreviations your students may need to know in the areas of (1) everyday life, including abbreviations used for specific purposes such as interpreting advertisements for jobs or housing and/or (2) academic life, including abbreviations used in reference materials such as library catalogs, bibliographies, indexes, and electronic databases as well as for the discussion of and writing of academic research.

Procedure for presenting common abbreviations: Write your selected abbreviations on the board and ask your students to write on paper the meanings of as many as they already know or can guess. Collect the papers and eliminate from your master list the abbreviations that all or most students already know. If you have time during the class, tell students the meanings of some of the abbreviations that few or none of them knew. Tell them that you will provide a list of the unfamiliar abbreviations and their meanings at the next class.

In preparation for the next class, make a list of the abbreviations that were new to most students: Include the abbreviation, its meaning, and an example and/or explanation of its use. Assign the study list to your students as homework.

At the following class, write the selected abbreviations on the board. Ask students to explain them without referring to their study lists.

Note: The following lists are intended as "starter" lists. You will want to expand them according to your students' needs and interests.

Examples of abbreviations likely to be found in common usage:

a.m. Example: 1:15 a.m.	before noon
ATM	automatic teller machine
CD-ROM	compact disk–read only memory
COD	cash on delivery
dept.	department
Dr.	doctor
etc.	and others
govt.	government
ID	identification
inc.; Inc.	including; incorporated
misc.	miscellaneous
mph	miles per hour
Mr.	mister (man's form of address)
Mrs.; Ms.	forms of address for women
No.	number
P.O.	post office
p.m.	after noon
Rd.	road
RR	railroad
St.	street
TBA	to be announced
TV	television
UN	United Nations
WWI (WWII)	the First (or Second) World War

Language-based activities

Note: Abbreviations for the days of the week, for the months, and, in the United States, for the states are also useful.

Examples of abbreviations likely to be found specifically in help wanted ads:

BA; BS	Bachelor of Arts; Bachelor of Science
exper or exp	experience; experienced
FT	full time
GED (General Education Diploma)	equivalent to U.S. high school diploma
hrs/wk	hours per week
HS	high school
M – F	Monday through Friday
PT	part time
req or req'd	required
temp	temporary
401K	a type of pension plan

Examples of abbreviations likely to be found specifically in real estate ads:

A/C	air conditioned
ap's applc'd	appliances; applianced
apt	apartment
av or avail	available
ba or BA	bathroom
br or BR	bedroom
flr	floor
gar	garage
ht	heat
h.w.	hot water
imm	immediate
refs	references
rfg or refrig	refrigerator
rms	rooms
sec. dep.	security deposit
s/f or sq. ft.	square feet
stv	stove
w&d or (W/D)	washer and dryer

Follow-up: Have students find employment or real estate ads (in newspapers, in supermarket flyers, copied from newspapers in the library) and bring them to class to write on the board.

When a number of ads have been displayed, have students decode each others' ads without using their study lists.

Students will probably find additional abbreviations or forms of abbreviations that are different from the ones given here.

Examples of abbreviations used for academic purposes:

A.D. used before a date: A.D. 300	in the Christian era
b. used before a date: b. 1955	born
B.C. used after a date: 17 B.C.	before Christ
c. or ca. an approximate date	circa (around)
d. used before a date: d. 1998	died
ed.	editor, edition, edited by
et al.	and others
e.g.	for example
i.e.	that is
n.d.	no date (of publication)
p.,pp.	page, pages (omit, preceding page numbers, unless needed for clarity)
pub. or publ.	publisher, publication, published by
qtd.	quoted
rev.	review or revision
vol.	volume

A.5.7 Don't believe everything you read

Learning to evaluate what one reads; working with implication, assumption, and possibility or probability.

Procedure: Draw a simple scene on the board such as the one shown here. Next, write some sentences on the board about your illustration.

Language-based activities

Sample sentences:

1. The dog is wearing a collar.
2. The dog is chasing a cat.
3. The dog is chasing three people.
4. One person has torn pants.

Ask students to determine which statements are verifiably true and which are false.

Then add some statements that cannot be verified by the illustration. For this illustration, for example, you could write:

5. The dog tore the man's pants.
6. The people wanted to pat the dog.

Use this illustration and these types of statements to address such subjects as implication, assumption, and probability or possibility.

Follow-up: Have students compose more statements of these types, and choose some to be written on the board to continue the activity.

A.6 Listening and/or speaking

Of the activities in this section, Activities A.6.1 and A.6.2 are about Listening, and Activities A.6.3 and A.6.4 are about Speaking. The rest of the activities involve students in both listening and speaking situations.

A helpful suggestion regarding dialogue read to the class for the purpose of practicing listening and speaking skills (as in Activity A.6.9) comes from Andrew Wright and Safia Haleem in *Visuals for the Language Classroom* (1991). They suggest drawing faces on the board to represent different speakers, and then pointing to the faces as you read.

A.6.1   Write the numbers
A.6.2   Similar or different?
A.6.3   Writing, illustrating, and performing dialogues and skits
A.6.4   Using the board in oral presentations
A.6.5   Giving and getting directions
A.6.6   Student dictation
A.6.7   Hamburger dictation
A.6.8   Constructing a jigsaw picture
A.6.9   Formal and informal speech

See also, for listening:

A.1.15 Let's go food shopping
A.2.2   Practicing stress patterns
A.2.7   Numbers ending in *-teen* and those ending in *-ty*

See also, for speaking:

A.4.5   Telling and writing a story
A.5.3   Read, illustrate, and retell
B.1.6   What we like to do or don't like to do (Br.E., like doing or don't like doing)
B.1.7   Personality sketches (introducing oneself)
B.1.9   My family tree (describing a relative)
B.1.10 A family adventure – a traditional story
B.1.11 Telling about one's country or culture
B.1.12 Comparing cultural differences: Time, relationships
B.1.13 Comparing cultural differences: Colors
B.2.5   Setting class, team, pair, or individual agendas (a speaking agenda)

Language-based activities

B.3.1   Scavenging for signs (students report on results of scavenger hunt)

B.3.2   Scavenging for answers (students report on results of scavenger hunt)

See also, for listening and speaking:

A.3.8   Modals: Possibility, obligation, and necessity (explaining how to play a game, taking notes during a presentation)

A.3.9   Question words (listening to and answering *wh-* questions)

A.3.13 Do you need any _____? (listening to and answering questions)

B.1.4   Where Irene lives (Follow-up: Students report on conversations with peers)

B.1.5   Hello, do you like to _____? (asking and answering yes and no and *wh-* questions)

B.1.8   Would I lie to you?

B.1.14 Planning a menu (sharing personal information)

B.1.15 A graphic view of who we are: A project (interviewing peers)

B.3.4   A message in a bottle (peer negotiation)

B.3.5   How does it rank? (peer group discussion)

B.3.6   How does it rate? (peer discussion and/or debate)

A.6.1 Write the numbers

Procedure: Divide your class into teams, each with three to five members, and appoint a scribe for each team. A team can help its scribe verbally but should not be permitted to write an answer on paper for the scribe to copy on the board.

Announce the type of numbers you will be dictating: dates, telephone numbers, prices, or measurements.

Call out the number and award a point to the team whose scribe first writes the number correctly.

Change scribes periodically so that other team members get a chance to do the board work.

Follow-up: Once students exhibit a fair amount of proficiency with one category of numbers, give them a random assortment of two or more categories such as the following:

1877; 1-800-555-8888
6 feet by 2 inches; 2½ liters
1616; $16.16; sixteen dollars and 16/100
Three thousand two hundred and ten miles; 12 kilometers
19th; nineteenth century

Variation: Have students practice writing both the numbers and the names of the numbers. For example, draw a check on the board, and have students fill in the numbers and written amounts you specify.

A.6.2 Similar or different?

Preparation: Find a text – perhaps one from your course book or use the sample text given here – in which two things are compared and contrasted.

Number the sentences and create a key that lists the appropriate sentence numbers under the headings similar and different. (The key to the sample passage appears at the end of the passage.)

Also, you may want to review comparison and contrast markers with your class before you proceed to the listening comprehension task.

Procedure: Divide your class into two groups, each with a scribe to do the board writing.

Mark off two columns on the board and leave space between them to give each scribe sufficient room to work. Mark one column *Similar* and the other one *Different,* and assign one scribe to each column. Explain to students that you will read numbered sentences that they

159

should listen to carefully in order to determine whether the sentence describes a similarity or a difference.

Scribes should write the numbers of the sentences that fit their heading in their column. Scribes can use their own best judgment, but members of their group may call out suggestions to them and may compose their own lists at their desks.

When you have finished reading, resolve any disagreements.

Finally, determine which group and which individual students have the most correct answers.

Sample text: Although Abraham Lincoln and John F. Kennedy, two of the most famous presidents of the United States, were very different in many ways, their lives demonstrate a striking number of similarities that many writers have noted. Some examples of both their similarities and their differences follow:

(1) Lincoln was born poor; Kennedy was born rich. (2) Lincoln was a Republican, but Kennedy was a Democrat. (3) They were both members of Congress when they were elected to the presidency. (4) Lincoln was elected in 1860, and Kennedy was elected in 1960. (5) Lincoln served as president during the Civil War, and Kennedy during the United States' military intervention in Vietnam.

(6) Both presidents married women who were more interested in society than in politics and who spoke French. (7) The Kennedys as well as the Lincolns suffered the death of a child.

(8) Both presidents were assassinated, and both assassins died soon after the assassinations. (9) Kennedy's assassin was assassinated; most people believe that Lincoln's took his own life. (10) All four men died from gunshots. (11) Lincoln was assassinated in the nation's capital; Kennedy was assassinated in Texas.

(12) The situations surrounding the assassinations were these: Lincoln was enjoying some personal time by attending a play; Kennedy, however, was on a political mission. (13) The men's wives were present when their husbands were killed. (14) Lincoln died in a boardinghouse across the street from the theater, whereas Kennedy died in a hospital. (15) A political associate of Lincoln was also wounded seriously, as was a political associate of Kennedy. (16) However, Kennedy's associate was injured because he was with Kennedy at the time, whereas Lincoln's associate was shot in his own home.

(17) Perhaps the most amazing point of comparison between the two politicians is that Lincoln's Vice-President Johnson and Kennedy's Vice-President Johnson succeeded the slain presidents.

160

Key:

Sentence No.	Similar	Different
	3	1
	4	2
	5	9
	6	11
	7	12
	8	14
	10	16
	13	
	15	
	17	

Comment: Depending on the level of your students' abilities, you may want to read each sentence more than once if students request it.

A.6.3 Writing, illustrating, and performing dialogues and skits

Procedure: Divide your class into small groups of two to four students, and have these groups write a dialogue to illustrate a grammar point or a communication strategy or to practice vocabulary associated with a specific topic you are working on – perhaps something based on a text or activity you are currently using in your course book.

Select the best dialogue for students to illustrate, and have the winning group read it aloud.

Next, ask another of the groups to draw a backdrop (scenery) on the board to illustrate the selected dialogue. If the dialogue contains different scenes, have other groups illustrate these scenes and draw props to accompany them. If you have colored chalk or markers available, you may want to choose one or more groups to draw and others to color the drawings.

Try to divide up the tasks so that all groups, even the winning group, are busy at the board at this point.

If your board space is inadequate, supplement it with newsprint; or have some students make individual drawings of props at their desk rather than on the board, to be used in the presentation of the dialogue as a skit.

Example:

Sample dialogue to accompany illustration on the preceding page:

Gretta: What do you think of this melon, Marin? Is it ripe?
Marin: Shake it. If you can hear the seeds moving inside, it's ripe.
Gretta: (*shaking melon*) OK. It rattles. Are you sure it's not too hard? Too soft? Does it smell rotten?
Marin: It's fine. Where's the clerk?
Clerk: May I help you?
Marin: Yes. We'd like the melon, please.
Clerk: (*weighing the melon*) That's $2.47.
Gretta: And how much is it without your finger on the scale?

Follow-ups:

1. Leave the illustration on the board, but form new groups of students so that writers of the winning dialogue are placed in different groups.
   Have students compose new dialogue to fit the illustration, and repeat the process.
2. Repeat the procedure using the dialogue written by the runner-up group.
3. Ask groups of students to draw backdrops and props on the board without a script. Try to have each group participate in the drawing, even if their space is small or they have to use the alternative materials mentioned above.
   Then have pairs or groups write dialogues about each other's illustrations and read and act them out using the scenery and props provided for them by their peers.

A.6.4   Using the board in oral presentations

Procedure: Assign oral presentations that narrate, explain, or teach something. These could be brief, informal presentations given to a student's small group or to the whole class. Or, they could be more extensive presentations given to a wider audience that might include another class or other teachers or friends and relatives of the students; to guests from the community such as sponsors of your program or residents of a local nursing home; or if you are teaching immigrant or international students, to a class of children from a community school who want to learn more about other countries and cultures.

Advise students to use the board, a flip chart, or overhead transparencies in their presentation, as an aid for themselves and for their audience by writing any or all of the following:

- A brief outline of the main points of their presentation, thus keeping both themselves and their audience focused.

163

- Key words, if there are technical terms or other specialized vocabulary in their presentations that may not be familiar to all members of their audience.
- Words they know they have trouble pronouncing. They can then point to the words at the appropriate time in their presentation if this becomes necessary.
- Their names, if some members of the audience do not know them.

Also suggest that they draw simple illustrations as they speak. This technique can be dynamic as well as very helpful. But if the graphic information is particularly important, they should reinforce it by preparing a handout that duplicates the board graphics and is done with the precision lacking in board writing.

A.6.5   Giving and getting directions

Procedure: Make up a map and draw it on the board. In a central location on the map, draw an X and label it *You Are Here.*

Draw a number of streets around the X and label them, using pairs of names composed of sounds that are difficult for your students to differentiate, for example, Prayer Street and Player Street. Also include houses and other buildings, statues, parks, and other landmarks and label them: the Volt house, the Bolt house, and so on.

You might want to use the map given here.

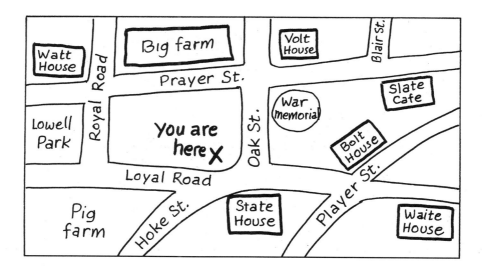

The actual drawing takes some time, so try to draw the map on the board before the class begins unless your students will be busy with some other activity while you are drawing it.

Have all your students choose where "their" house is located on the map and then have them write directions to "their" house on a piece of paper. They must use the names of streets and landmarks and not descriptions such as *the second street down from the top*.

Call on one student to read to the class the directions to her or his house. The other students should make notes from the directions given. They may also ask questions about the directions.

The student who has given directions then calls on a listener to go to the board and point to the location of the direction giver's house. If the listener points to an incorrect location, the direction giver keeps calling on other students until someone points to the correct location. That student then reads his or her directions aloud so that all the listeners can verify the accuracy of their notes.

Finally, the direction giver chooses a peer to take her or his place, and the procedure is repeated.

Comment: If your students have a limited vocabulary for giving directions, you might want to review some appropriate phrases such as *go straight, turn left (or right),* and *go past (or across).*

If you have a large class, divide it into pairs, having one student write the directions and the other read them.

A.6.6 Student dictation

Preparation: Select a narrative passage from a course book that contains material suitable for reading aloud. You may wish to select this passage from something recently read for homework or used in class.

Procedure: Ask a student to scan the passage as preparation for dictating it, while you send three or more students to the board to write. Other students write at their desks.

Tell students to write exactly what they hear. Explain that the activity has the following purposes: (1) to help the reader improve pronunciation, (2) to help writers improve their ability to determine whether something sounds right, and (3) to help writers improve their ability to question doubtful utterances or to repair them.

Encourage dialogue between the student who is dictating and the students who are writing so that they will try to resolve any difficulties. The student dictating may decide to spell the words the listeners cannot understand. Discourage this as an initial strategy, but if the frustration level rises, you may wish to permit it.

At the end of the dictation, instruct the students who wrote on the board to read carefully what they have written and to correct any remaining errors. Be sure that at least one of the board writers has achieved a correct version of the dictation. If no one has a correct version, have the student who dictated correct one of the public versions.

Comment: The student reader not familiar with dictation will need instruction in how to read. You may want to demonstrate reading in units such as phrases and clauses, slowly and clearly; pausing between units as long as students are writing; repeating each unit once or twice depending on its length and difficulty; and, at the end, repeating the entire passage once at a fairly normal rate of speech.

Variations for all levels:

1. Divide the reading material so that several students can have the opportunity to dictate it. Copy it, if possible giving each student in your class one or two sentences to read. Use numbered sheets of paper and call on students to read in sequence.

2. Or, instead of reading the coherent paragraph or passage as it was written, call on students to read out of sequence, thus forcing the writers to rely more on their understanding of the dictator's pronunciation for comprehension rather than on context and inference, thus increasing the chances that meaningful negotiation will occur. Or, choose discrete sentences as the basis for the dictation instead of a paragraph or passage.

3. Or, instead of having several students write the whole dictation publicly, have one student write the entire dictation.

   If the student doesn't understand a word or phrase, have him or her draw a blank line for the missing word(s).

   When the dictation is complete, call on other students to fill in the blanks; also have them underline any errors in the board work with a different color of chalk or marker.

   Keep sending students to the board until all blanks are filled in and all errors corrected, but do not permit the student who read the dictation to do any of this work unless all else fails.

Variation for lower levels: For lower levels, write key words at the top or at one side of the board.

Variations for advanced levels: Have each student write an original, short paragraph about a topic the class has recently explored or any topic that interests the student, to use as a dictation. Select or have students select one or several of these paragraphs to be used, as time permits, for future dictations.

A.6.7 Hamburger dictation

Role playing: Ordering food.

Procedure: Have students name some foods and drinks they like to order in a restaurant.

Write or have a scribe write these items in "menu form" on the board:

Example:

Sandwiches	*Side orders*	*Drinks*
Hamburger	French fries	Coffee
Chicken	Salad	Tea
Cheese	Fresh fruit (seasonal)	Milk
Peanut butter and jelly	Baked beans	Coca-Cola
Vegetarian	Rice	

Have each student write on a piece of paper what they want to "order" from the menu.

Then call on one student to be the "customer" and have her or him recite or read his or her order. The order may include special instructions such as *with mustard, white bread, toasted,* and *coffee with cream and sugar,* which you may also need to have students list on the board.

As the customer orders, each of the other students writes the order on a piece of paper.

When the customer has finished ordering, she or he calls on one student to act as the "server." This student may now ask the customer questions or ask for clarification of items.

The server then goes to the board, verifies the order by reading aloud what she or he has written, and, if an item is correct, ticks it off on the board list so that all the students can check their lists for accuracy.

Finally, the customer chooses another student to take her or his role, and the procedure is repeated with a different student being asked, after the order has been placed, to take the role of server.

Comments: This activity works well as a beginning experience with dictation because the words are publicly displayed and the listeners can focus on finding the words they hear and copying them correctly.

If your students' pronunciation is still very problematic, you may want to read their orders for them. If your students need help forming requests and asking for clarification, write some prompts on the board; for example, Could I have some _____ ? Do you have any _____ ? Did you say you wanted _____ ?

167

Follow-up: After several students have dictated and responded, you may want to continue the activity in small groups if your students are able to read their own orders sufficiently clearly.

A.6.8 Constructing a jigsaw picture

Preparation: On a sheet of paper, draw a picture using simple geometric shapes such as those used to produce the examples shown here.
Examples:

  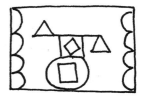

Because you will be describing your picture for some students to draw on the board and others to draw at their desks, you will need paper for those working at their desks. In addition, if you wish to include color, you will need colored chalk or markers for students using the board, and crayons or colored pencils for students at their desks.

Before you begin to describe your picture, you may need to introduce and/or write some key vocabulary words on the board such as:

• Geometric forms: triangle, square, rectangle, circle
• Prepositions: across, between, inside
• Adjectives: horizontal, vertical, upper, lower
• Nouns: corner, edge.

Procedure: Send some students to the board, and have each one draw a frame for her or his picture.

Then describe your picture, telling students step-by-step what figure to draw, how large to draw it, and where to place it. For example, draw a small rectangle and place it one quarter of the way down from the top and one eighth of the way in from the right edge of your frame.

If students do not understand your directions, allow them to ask specific questions such as, "Where should we draw the rectangle?" or "Did you say to draw a square or a rectangle?" Do not allow them simply to ask you to repeat.

When you have finished describing your drawing, and all the discrepancies in the students' re-creations have been resolved, have students at their desks take turns dictating impromptu additions to the picture by first having them draw an addition on their copy of the picture and then having them tell the other students what to draw.

Follow-up: After students are familiar with the exercise, ask each one to prepare his or her own drawing – this could be done as a homework assignment – and to dictate it to the class, to a partner, or to a small group.

Comment: Constructing a jigsaw picture publicly has an advantage over the more traditional method in which the results are not viewed until the end of the presentation because we can observe students' comprehension problems as they occur and we can correct them immediately. Also, students can observe when the drawings at the board differ. Thus, they can participate more actively in discussion with the presenter and with each other about the directions being given.

A.6.9   Formal and informal speech

Contrastive analysis of word choice, grammar, and pronunciation in (American) spoken formal and informal English.

Procedure: In order to provide a vehicle for analyzing and discussing differences in formal and informal communication, begin by writing on the board, side-by-side, if possible, two short dialogues, one using formal language and the other informal language, such as the ones that follow:

Dialogue A:

S1: Hello. This is Howard Bluestone. How are you?
S2: Fine, thank you. And you?
S1: Just fine, thanks. Could we discuss that account now?
S2: I'm really very sorry, but I can't just now. May I get back to you?
S1: Yes, I'll be here until 5 this afternoon, or you can call me tomorrow.

Dialogue B:

S1: Hey, how're you doin'?
S2: Good. How 'bout you?
S1: Not bad. Wanna play some ball?
S2: Maybe later.

   Read the dialogues to the students; then ask them questions about each one such as:

• What do you think is the relationship between the speakers?
• What is the topic of conversation?
• Can you tell whether they are speaking over the phone or face-to-face?

- Is the language formal or informal? Have students think about features such as the use of slang, contractions, grammar, pronunciation, degrees of politeness.
- What specific elements in the dialogue tell you that it is formal or informal?

Using a different-colored chalk or marker from the one used to write the dialogues, write students' comments under the dialogues and circle or underline features in the dialogues that led to the students' conclusions.

Be sure that students become aware that the differences in the two dialogues are not only in the words chosen and their forms (the lexicon), the grammar, and the pronunciation, but that there are also sociolinguistic factors such as the relationship of the speakers, their reason(s) for speaking, and possibly even their mode of communicating.

Follow-up or homework: Have students write pairs of dialogues illustrating formal and informal spoken communication.

Then select some for students to copy on the board.

Have the writers read their dialogues aloud and describe the formal and informal elements they have used.

Conclude with whole-class discussion.

Acknowledgment: The idea for this activity comes from Andrew Wright and Safia Haleem, *Visuals for the Language Classroom* (1991).

A.7 General reviewing and assessing

In addition to the activities in this section, listed below, many activities in other sections of this book ask that students review a concept or skill. Therefore, many activities in this book provide a means for assessing whether students have understood a concept or mastered a skill.

There are, in fact, too many such activities to include in the "See also" list below, although I have noted two of the most useful ones there.

A.7.1 Targeting correct language use: Vocabulary, pronunciation, or grammar
A.7.2 Right or wrong?
A.7.3 Recall review
A.7.4 What I learned from today's class; questions I have about today's material

See also:

A.1.24 Reviewing and assessing new vocabulary
B.2.2 Keeping score (assessing progress in language acquisition or assessing improvement of academic behavior)

A.7.1 Targeting correct language use: Vocabulary, pronunciation, or grammar

Encouraging the use of, assessing, and rewarding correct language usage.

Preparation: Draw a large target on the board in a spot where you can leave it for several class periods, if possible.

Procedure for vocabulary work:

1. Choose four to six words that you have already introduced, defined, and discussed in your class and that you want your students to be able to generate in their speech or writing. Write these words around the outside of the target.
2. When a student correctly uses one of the target words, write her or his name in the outer ring of the target. Use an arrow to indicate the student's ongoing success using the target word until, with the fourth success, the student's name enters the bull's-eye!

Example:

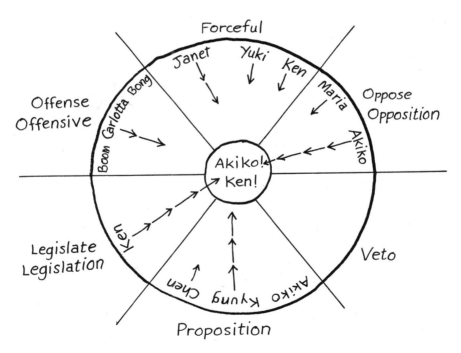

Procedure for pronunciation work: Select a phoneme that is troublesome for your students, for example, a specific vowel sound not found in their first language, *-ed* endings, final *-s,* or other final consonants. Or use the distinction between voiced and voiceless *th,* between /b/ and /p/, or between /l/ and /r/. If the first languages of your students vary, you may want to create individual targets. Have students select the phonemes they believe are most difficult for them. Label the target with the phoneme(s) on which you want students to focus.

Listen during class discussion or reading-aloud activities for occasions when students successfully articulate a target phoneme. Then follow step 2 above.

Procedure for grammar work: Select a grammar structure on which you want your students to focus, for example, using correct word order in *wh-,* yes/no, and tag questions or using past tense verbs correctly. Label the target with the structures you've chosen and follow step 2.

Comment: If you cannot leave your target(s) on the board for more than one class period, you can make a copy on newsprint and tack it to your bulletin board.

Keeping target language usage on display and presenting it in a competitive but fun way motivates students to use the new language over a period of time, which is exactly what it takes to commit new words – their meanings and/or their pronunciation – and new grammatical structures to long-term memory.

This technique also enables students to assess their own progress and simplifies your assessment tasks.

Scorekeeping is not a burden because students can be encouraged to record their successes themselves if you are busy or don't notice.

A.7.2 Right or wrong?

Checking answers.

Procedure: Have students use the board as a way to check multiple-choice, true-false, and other short-answer exercises they have done for homework or in class, or even to check short answers to quizzes or tests.

Ask volunteers to put answers on the board; involve as many students as you can. Let the volunteers determine which question(s) they want to answer – they will avoid ones in which they lack confidence, and few wrong answers will be written. Usually observers will point out any wrong answers and students will make corrections themselves.

If problems or questions remain for you to deal with, however, it probably means that this part of the work being tested needs further elaboration and/or review.

When all the correct answers are displayed, students can grade their own papers, or they can grade each other's.

Comment: Having students provide answers and correct errors – typically "teacher acts" – helps to empower students.

Variation: If time is limited, write correct answers on the board for students to self-check.

A.7.3 Recall review

Providing a summary of a class to emphasize important concepts and to help fix these concepts in students' memories.

Procedure: At the end of a class or a series of classes in which important concepts have been presented, ask students to recall the major concepts. Write the concepts on the board. If students omit important concepts, add them.

Follow-up: If time permits, ask questions about each concept to find out how much students have understood and remembered.

A.7.4 What I learned from today's class; questions I have about today's material

Procedure: At the end of class, give students a few minutes to write responses to the following:

1. What did you learn in class today? Be specific!
2. What more do you want to know, or what didn't you understand, if anything, about the material we covered in class today?

Be sure that students are very specific in responding to the first question. In other words, they should *not* write: "I learned a spelling rule." Rather, they should write the rule itself.

When students have finished writing, quickly look over their responses to the first question, and then select as many different answers as you can and write them on the board. This provides a quick review and at least a partial summary of the day's classwork.

Follow-up: Then, in preparation for your next class, look over the students' responses to your second question. This will allow you to assess how well students grasped any new concepts you have presented. Actually, their responses to the first question often permit you to assess their understanding as well, because sometimes what they think they "learned" is not the same as what you thought you taught!

If several students have questions about the same concept, write the question on the board and use it as a starting point for your next class.

If some students have written questions you prefer not to display publicly, write your answers on their papers and return them at the next class.

Acknowledgment: I was introduced to the basic concept of asking students to write what they have learned and what they want to know at the end of every class as a teacher in the Institute for English Language (IEL) program at Harvard University. The technique is a tradition throughout the university.

B Content-based activities

B.1 Getting acquainted and building community

The purpose of these activities is to provide an active way for us as teachers to get to know our students and for our students to get to know each other and us. Thus, Activities B.1.1 through B.1.3, good icebreakers, draw out students' names and countries; Activities B.1.4 through B.1.8 as well as B.1.15 help students learn about each others' lives and personalities; Activities B.1.9 and B.1.10 relate to family; and Activities B.1.11 through B.1.14 relate to culture.

B.1.1   What's my name?
B.1.2   Getting to know you
B.1.3   Where I was born, where I live, where I have traveled; places in the news
B.1.4   Where Irene lives
B.1.5   Hello, do you like to ___?
B.1.6   What we like to do or don't like to do (Br.E., like doing or don't like doing)

Students from the author's ESL class at Southern New Hampshire University celebrating Halloween, October 1996.

Content-based activities

B.1.7   Personality sketches
B.1.8   Would I lie to you?
B.1.9   My family tree
B.1.10 A family adventure – a traditional story
B.1.11 Telling about one's country or culture
B.1.12 Comparing cultural differences: Time, relationships
B.1.13 Comparing cultural differences: Colors
B.1.14 Planning a menu
B.1.15 A graphic view of who we are: A project

See also:

A.1.13 Naming: Colors, parts of the body, and clothing (an icebreaking
        activity)
A.5.2   Filling out forms (personal information used on applications)

B.1.1 What's my name?

Using drawings to "write" names.

Procedure: Model this activity for your students by "writing" your name on the board using a drawing of an object to represent each letter. My name, for example, would look like this:

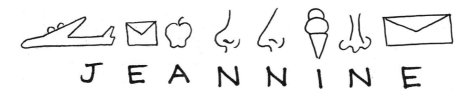

Challenge students to decipher your name and then invite them to portray their names on the board in a like manner. Give students time to think and perhaps make a preliminary sketch at their seats.

Then, if your class is not too large, have students go to the board one at a time and have the whole class work out the letters for each one's name.

If your class is large, you may want all the students to display their names on the board to begin with. Even a large class, however, can probably do this in a moderate amount of board space if some students draw above, and some below, others, although you may have to send them to the board in shifts. Then see how many names students can decipher within a certain time limit – say 10 minutes.

Once the time is up, have volunteers write their interpretations of the names on the board and have the owners of the names make corrections, if needed. If any names remain undeciphered, have the whole class work on them until everyone's name has been determined.

B.1.2 Getting to know you

Learning students' names and, for multilingual students, countries.

Preparation: Before your first meeting with a new class of students, draw a picture on the board that matches your classroom seating arrangement. See the example on the next page.

Procedure: If you teach multilingual students, as class begins, call on each student to go to the board and write his or her name and country of origin in the box that corresponds to his or her seat.

If you teach monolingual students, have them write their name and also draw or write a mnemonic aid that represents their name to make

it easier to remember. For my name – Jeannine – for example, I might
write *Jean9*.

Example:

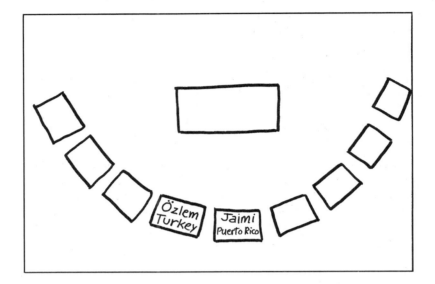

After each student has participated, continue with verbal
introductions, icebreaker activities (see Activity B.1.3, for example), or
whatever you normally plan for first class meetings with new students.

If possible, leave the chart on the board throughout the first class or
until you and your students learn each others' names.

Variation: Instead of writing their countries' names or a mnemonic aid
after their names, have students write or just say something about
themselves such as a nickname, a goal, an achievement, or their
favorite animal, celebrity, activity, or food.

B.1.3 Where I was born, where I live, where I have traveled; places in the news

Procedure: If your students come from different countries, ask them to
imagine that the board contains a map of the world. Have them write
their name and the name of the city where they were born or where
they now live (in their *own* country) at the proper place on the "map,"
but don't let them actually draw their country on the board. Keep the
map imaginary.

Example:

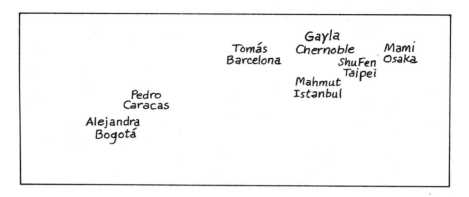

Students will soon discover that they need first to discuss their response with their classmates to determine where on the imaginary map they should write.

If your students all come from the same country or town and speak the same first language, have them imagine that the board is that country or town. Encourage them to hold their discussion in English.

Variation: Have students write in the names of places in the world they have visited or would like to visit or that have been in the news during the past year.

Comment: To prevent confusion, be sure that students are aware that in maps of the Western Hemisphere Europe and Africa are placed at the center of the world and in maps of the Eastern Hemisphere Asia is placed at the center.

If your own geography is rusty, you might want to have a map on hand so that you can serve as a resource when the students need help.

Acknowledgment: This activity is based on one by Lori Lalonda, "Dave's ESL Cafe: Dave's ESL Idea Page." <www.eslcafe.com> (July 20, 1997).

B.1.4 Where Irene lives

Eliciting personal information as material for a drill (in this case, a drill of verb agreement following the constructions *there is . . ./there are . . .*); vocabulary building.

Procedure: Begin by asking one student to volunteer. Afterward, students work in pairs so that each student gets a chance to share information. Elicit information from the student regarding where he or she lives.

As the student provides the information, rephrase it correctly in a complete sentence if need be, and then draw a picture on the board to represent key words or key ideas the student has provided.

As each piece of information is completed, point to its picture, using it as a prompt for the students to repeat the dialogue singly and/or in unison.

Example

T: Do you live in an apartment building or in a house?
S: Apartment building.
T: Irene lives in an apartment building.

Draw an apartment building on the board (see the first illustration shown on the next page).

Then point to the drawing and, if you have a small class, call on each student to repeat the dialogue and then have the class as a whole repeat it. If you have a large class, call on specific students and then have the whole class repeat it.

Next ask, "How many rooms are there in your apartment?" When the student replies, draw a floor plan to represent the answer, point to it, and repeat the student's information, but use a *there is . . ./there are . . .* construction: "There are three rooms in Irene's apartment."

Have students repeat the dialogue.

As time permits, continue asking questions such as, "Do you have a rug in your living room?" "What furniture is in your living room?" "What is in your bedroom?" "Your kitchen?" and so on, following the procedure described above each time the student answers.

Once you have elicited a number of answers, point to each picture you have drawn on the board and ask individual students or the whole class to repeat the dialogue in answer to questions such as, "Who can say what furniture there is in Irene's bedroom?" "Who can say what there is in the kitchen?"

When the story is complete, students may practice the dialogues in pairs or small groups.

They may also copy the pictures on one sheet of paper and write out the dialogue on another. In this way, they can use the pictures later to try to re-create the dialogues from memory and use the written dialogue to check their accuracy.

Follow-up: Students work in pairs, asking each other where they live and what is to be found in each of their rooms.

Students draw pictures of their partners' answers.

Students report to the whole class what their partners have told them.

If you have a large class, students may have to report in small groups rather than to the whole class.

Acknowledgment: The method described here is put forth by Norma Shapiro and Carol Genser in *Chalk Talks* (illustrated by Genser; 1994). I have created this activity based on Shapiro's model and on Genser's Dictionary of Symbols contained in the book.

B.1.5 Hello, do you like to _____ ?

Asking and answering yes/no and *wh-* questions.

Procedure:

1. Write a list of activities on the board, as shown on the next page, leaving space under each one where names can be written.
2. Have students copy the list on a sheet of paper and circulate among their classmates asking, "Do you like to _____ ?" If they get a yes answer, they ask the answerers their names, which they write on their list.
3. Then have students ask the answerers a related question such as, "What sport do you play?" "What kinds of food do you cook?" "Where do you shop?"
4. Finally, when they have completed their conversation, have them enter the answerers' names on the appropriate line on the board and then take another question to continue the process. Or they can become an answerer for another student's questions.

Content-based activities

Example:

dance	cook	travel	sing	shop	read	play a sport	study
YanFei	Yuri	Sukru	Fred	Sukru		Sukru	Aman
		Emir	Yuki	Alejandra	Aman		
				Nick			

If the student's name has already been entered on the board for a particular category, it cannot be written in again.

The questioner must ask others the question or move to a new question.

While students are conducting their interviews, you can circulate and listen for errors in how students formulate their *wh-* questions.

5. When time is up for information gathering, discuss some of the more popular and less popular responses written on the board and ask students to share the additional information they gathered from their peers.

Acknowledgment: This activity is based on one in Laurel Pollard and Natalie Hess, *Zero Prep: Ready to Go Activities for the Language Classroom* (1997).

B.1.6   What we like to do or don't like to do (Br.E., like doing or don't like doing)

Sharing personal information while practicing the grammatical constructions *like + verb, both* or *and, neither* or *nor*.

Procedure for small classes: Ask students, at their seats or at the board, to list a number of activities they like.

On the board, draw a table so that each student is represented, and choose five or six activities from a number of the students' lists to enter on it. Have students tell you what activities they like, and record their data.

Example:

	Jo Jo	Emil	Gunter	Bong	P.K.
Read	X			X	
Draw	X	X			
Sing		X			X
Cook	X				X
Travel	X	X	X	X	
Play sports		X	X	X	X

Next, ask questions such as, "Who likes to cook?" to elicit responses such as, "Jo Jo and P.K. like to cook." Then introduce the grammatical construction *Both* Jo Jo *and* P. K. like to cook. Or ask, "Do Gunter and Bong like to sing?" "No, *neither* Gunter *nor* Bong likes to sing."
Variations:

1. Use other topics such as places, foods, TV programs, songs we like to sing or listen to.
2. Follow the same procedure for activities or other topics that the students *dislike*.

Procedure for large classes: Draw the table on the board, using it as a model to explain this activity to your whole class. Then divide your class into small groups of five or six students.

Assign each group a different topic, perhaps using some of the topics suggested under Variations above. Have one member of each group record the group's data.

Taking one group at a time, have a member transfer the group's data to the board. Illustrate the grammatical constructions using each group's data.

B.1.7 Personality sketches

Relating adjectives to personality traits.

Procedure if all students have board space: Divide up the available board space so that each student has a section in which to draw.

Instruct students to draw a "collage" that shows them (using a stick figure) involved in an activity they love or that is representative of their personality, surrounded by items that reveal their hobbies, interests, future goals, and the like.

Have them title and sign their drawings.

Finally, under their drawings have the students write a list of adjectives describing the personality traits they have portrayed in the collage.

Example:

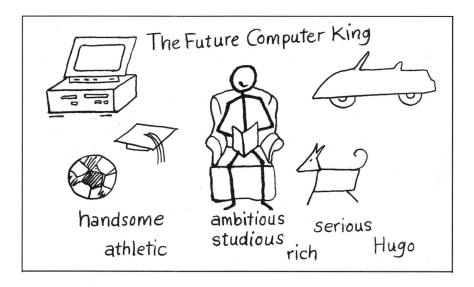

When the board work is completed, have students take turns going to the board, introducing themselves and explaining their drawings, personalities, goals, and so on.

Follow-up: Leave the drawings on the board but erase the adjectives and challenge students to restore them. Of course, the subject of a drawing cannot participate in restoring his or her own adjectives.

Variation: Instead of having the illustrators list their personality traits, have their peers guess what these traits might be, based on the sketches, and write – or have a scribe write – the adjectives under the drawings.

Procedure for large classes and/or limited board space: Divide your class into several small groups.

Have students draw at their desks according to the directions given above, but do not have them list adjectives describing their personality traits.

Have each group select one or two of its members, depending on board space available, to duplicate their drawings on the board.

While these students are doing this board work, have the others exchange their drawings and try to guess what personality traits or adjectives the illustrators had in mind.

Then have the class do the same for the board illustrations.

B.1.8   Would I lie to you?

Procedure: Select a student to write on the board three brief but complete sentences about him or herself – two statements that are true and one that is false.

Students at their desks take turns asking the writer for more information about each of the three statements to try to determine which one is the lie.

The writer can make up answers about the false statements but must tell the truth about the true ones. For example, I might write:

1. I have ridden in a hot air balloon.
2. I have ridden on a dog sled.
3. I have fallen out of a boat.

The lie is number 2. When asked where I rode on the dog sled, I could lie and say Alaska. But when asked about Alaska or dog sleds, for example, my lack of real knowledge would soon become apparent. (Students often ask sharp questions, and making up information on the spot can be difficult to do!)

Once a student thinks that she or he knows which statement is the lie, she or he cannot directly ask the writer whether the statement is true or false and cannot merely guess which statement is false but must give a reason why she or he thinks the statement is a lie. Thus, a student might say to me, "I think number 2 is the lie because you said that sled dogs eat dog food and I think they eat raw meat." Whether or not the student's reasoning is correct, if she or he chooses the lie and gives a logical reason for believing that it is a lie, she or he will have the next turn at the board.

Students who have already had a turn at the board can continue to ask questions. However, if they determine which statement is the lie, they cannot take another turn at the board. Instead, they should choose a student who has not yet written at the board to do so.

If a student makes two incorrect choices, leaving only the lie, the writer should call on a student who has not yet written at the board to take a turn.

Comment: Sentences that begin with *I have . . .* (meaning *I have done something* or *I possess something*), *I like to . . .*, and *I can . . .* work well.

You might want to model this activity, not only to give students some ideas about what to write but to contribute to the spirit of getting acquainted by supplying some personal information about yourself.

B.1.9 My family tree

Preparation: Draw your family tree on the board for students to use as a model.

Procedure: Divide your class into groups of three to five students.

Students should construct their own family tree, labeling the relationship of each member of their family to themselves, using your family tree or mine, which follows, as their model.

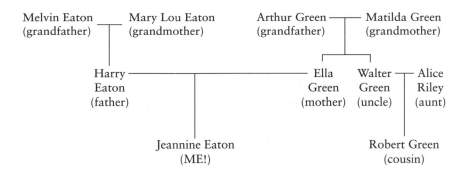

Next, ask students to consider which member of their family tree is the most special, interesting, unusual, or famous. Ask them to make a short oral presentation to the members of their group describing this relative and what makes him or her special, interesting, unusual, or famous.

Finally, have each group select one student to display his or her family tree on the board and to present a short, oral report to the whole class describing one relative's relationship to him or her – father, aunt, nephew – and relating the qualities or anecdotes that make that relative special.

Comment: If trees get too complicated, permit students to simplify, which I have done on the preceding page.

B.1.10   A family adventure – a traditional story

Procedure: Divide your class into small groups.

Have students tell the members of their group about an adventure they have had with their family.

Each group then votes on which one of their members should display his or her adventure on the board.

Winning students draw a scene on the board to illustrate their adventure.

Then classmates in the other groups try to guess what happened in the adventure. If this proves to be too difficult, have the illustrator add balloon dialogue for the people in the pictures or add labels to objects or give the picture a title or, as a last resort, add verbal details and give verbal hints.

Finally, have each student summarize his or her adventure.

Comment: To keep everybody busy while the winning students are drawing publicly, have the remaining students draw their adventure on paper or write a short summary of it to post around the room at the end of the activity.

Variation for multilingual classes: If your students come from different countries, have them use a story that is traditional in their culture instead of, or perhaps at a later time in addition to, a family adventure.

Follow-up: Have other students invent and tell stories using the existing public drawings.

B.1.11 Telling about one's country or culture

Procedure for multilingual classes: If your students come from different countries, have them each plan a presentation in which they use the board to help them teach something about their country or culture.

If some of your students are from the same country, have them work together on the larger topics.

For example, ask students to do the following work on the board:

1. Draw their country's flag and explain what its features (colors, symbols) stand for.
2. Draw the shape of their country and insert the names of major cities,

Students in the author's Intensive English Program class at the American Language and Culture Center at Southern New Hampshire University help each other with their board writing (October 2000).

explaining why they're famous and/or important. If their country is large, ask them to:

   a. Explain what the terrain looks like.

   b. Explain what the weather is like in the various regions.

   c. Mark where important historical events occurred. Draw objects that symbolize the events and label them.

3. Draw (and color) an example of a traditional dress worn for a special occasion, explain the occasion, and tell what someone wearing the outfit would be doing. An American, for example, might explain that some people in the United States dress as a ghost, witch, or scary monster for Halloween.

4. Explain the significance of specific colors in their culture. Use the appropriate colored chalk or marker to write with. An American, for example, might use red to draw and label a Valentine heart, black for the word *funeral* or *death,* or green for *jealousy.* (For a variation on this step of this activity involving the whole class, see Activity B.1.13.)

5. Write a recipe on the board and explain how to prepare a traditional dish. (Also see Activity B.1.14.)

6. Do one or more of the following: Draw and label types of architecture, famous buildings or monuments, types of transportation used, or animals, insects, flowers, trees, and so on, found in their country.

Procedure for monolingual classes: If your students come from the same country, have them each plan a presentation that reveals something about their personalities, their families, or their lives.

For example, ask students to:

1. Write a recipe for their favorite dish on the board and explain how to prepare it.
2. Draw a picture of where they live: the outside of the building, the surrounding area, a floor plan, and/or a map to use to describe to classmates the location of their dwelling place in relationship to local landmarks or the like.
3. Draw a picture of a favorite place and its surroundings and/or mark its location on a map to use to describe to classmates what makes it special and/or how to get there.
4. Draw a scene from a favorite book or story to use to describe the scene or book to classmates and to explain why it appeals to them.
5. Draw a scene that represents a special event in their lives. Draw the objects that symbolize the event (a religious event, a special birthday, a trip, a wedding, the birth of a child, a graduation, receiving a special gift, winning an important game), and use the drawing to describe the event for the class.
6. Draw (and color) an outfit they wore for a very special occasion and explain and describe the occasion for the class.

B.1.12 Comparing cultural differences: Time, relationships

Procedure for immigrant or international students: Draw a grid on the board. Allow a column for each of your student's cultures and one for your own.

Pose a question and then fill in the grid with an abbreviation for each answer.

Examples: Time: It is OK to be late if the person you keep waiting is. . . .

	Ecuador	India	Japan	Korea	Thailand	United States
A close friend						Maybe
A close relative						Maybe

	Ecuador	India	Japan	Korea	Thailand	United States
An acquaintance						N
Older than you						N
Younger than you						N
An employer						N
An employee						N
A teacher						N
A person of authority						N
A public official						N

In the following cases, you should arrive a little ahead of time (A), on time (O), a little late (L):

	Ecuador	India	Japan	Korea	Thailand	United States
A job interview						A
Work						A/O
A lecture or class						A
A meeting, or concert						A/O

B.1 Getting acquainted and building community

It is OK to be _____ minutes late in the following cases:

	Ecuador	India	Japan	Korea	Thailand	United States
A job interview						0
Work						0
A lecture or class						0
A meeting or concert						0
A date with a friend						0
A party						15–30

Variations:

- To explore *male and female roles,* ask questions such as, "Who in your family, other than servants (if any), usually (1) prepares meals, (2) washes clothes, (3) shops, (4) votes, (5) drives a car, (6) works outside the home, (7) cares for children, or (8) attends public functions?"
- To discuss *academic relationships:* "When you are a student, is it appropriate or not appropriate to do the following: (1) arrive late to class, (2) do friends' work for them, (3) use other people's ideas or words without acknowledgment, (4) give teachers expensive gifts to influence grades, (5) ask teachers for extra help, (6) ask teachers for letters of recommendation, (7) question the teacher, (8) express your own opinion, or (9) raise your hand to be called upon?"
- To discuss *host and guest relationships:* "When you are a guest in another person's home, is it appropriate or not appropriate to do the following: (1) bring a gift for your host, (2) help the host cook, (3) take the best chair or food, (4) help the host clean up or make your own bed, (5) change the TV channel, (6) charge phone calls to the host, (7) correct the host's children, (8) feed the host's pets unasked, or (9) write a thank-you note?"

Comment: If your students are from very diverse cultures, this activity may take more time than might at first appear necessary because it can elicit considerable discussion.

Variation for monolingual EFL students: Follow the procedure above, comparing your students' culture with the English-speaking culture you are from or with which you are familiar.

B.1.13 Comparing cultural differences: Colors

For immigrant or international students: sharing information about cultures so that students better understand themselves, their peers, and their new environment.

Procedure: The fact that colors have symbolic meanings and associations is probably universal; however, what a color symbolizes or what meaning we attach to a color depends on our culture.

To elicit discussion of these cultural differences, draw a grid on the board. Allow a column for each student's culture and one for your own. Fill in the grid with each culture's response to various colors.

Example:

	Ecuador	India	Japan	Korea	Thailand	United States
Green						Jealousy, go, money, ecology, youth
Red						Danger, excitement, stop, heat, anger
Yellow						Caution, cowardice
White						Purity, innocence, coldness, death
Black						Evil, death
Blue						Sadness, baby boys, sky
Pink						Baby girls, sweetness

Comment: As with the previous activity, this one may take more time than might at first appear necessary because it may elicit considerable discussion.

B.1.14 Planning a menu

Sharing personal information (and, for multilingual students, cultural information).

Procedure for monolingual students: Divide your class into three or more groups of students.

Have each group brainstorm to determine some of the foods they like to eat.

Then have each group plan a lunch or dinner menu and write the menus and the ingredients used on the board.

Next, as time and the students' levels of ability permit, discuss such matters as nutrition (perhaps with an illustration on the board such as the one shown on the next page); compatibility of the foods in terms of taste, color, and texture; and possible substitute ingredients that might be used if the required ingredients are not available.

Then have the class as a whole look over the menus for the purpose of constructing a single, well-balanced menu that includes, if possible, at least one dish from each group's suggested menu.

Finally, have all the students vote on the various dishes, choosing one for each course.

Circle the dishes that have been chosen or erase the ones that have not been chosen.

Procedure for multilingual students: Divide your class according to the countries or areas of the world from which they come, and have each group brainstorm to determine some of the foods they typically eat.

Then follow the procedure described above for monolingual students, except that when the students vote on the final menu, they should also take into consideration the country of origin of the dish so that as many different countries are represented as possible.

Follow-up: The ideal follow-up is, of course, to assign groups of students to be responsible for preparing the dishes and to eat the food!

Comment: If you have a large class or lack sufficient board space or time, you may have to be content with having groups plan a one-dish meal.

Illustration: If you are teaching in the United States or teaching American culture, you may want to draw the widely used food pyramid that graphically displays the six basic food groups according to the proportions that U.S. nutritionists recommend be included in one's diet (as shown on the next page).

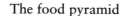

The food pyramid

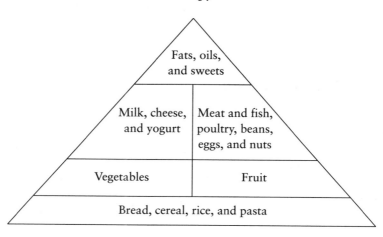

B.1.15 A graphic view of who we are: A project

Interviewing, gathering data, and constructing charts; using results of a survey to open dialogues for the purpose of getting better acquainted.

Preparation: Prepare a list of appropriate questions for students to ask each other in a personal interview. Prepare as many questions as you have students; or, for a large class, prepare half that many and have students work in pairs so that each student or each pair of students has one question to ask all the other students.

Examples for most students:

1. Do you have any pet dogs? cats? birds? fish? other pets?
2. Which do you like best: red, blue, green, yellow, or black?
3. What is your favorite way to travel: car? airplane? train? boat?
4. What kind of music do you like best: rock? pop? country and western? classical?
5. Which city would you like to visit: Washington, D.C.? Paris, France? Tokyo, Japan? Lima, Peru? Sydney, Australia? Johannesburg, South Africa?
6. Which is your favorite flower: rose? orchid? daisy? sunflower? other?
7. Which sport do you play: baseball? soccer? tennis? basketball? other? none?
8. What is your favorite fruit: apple? banana? orange? kiwi? peach? melon? other?
9. In which month were you born?
10. Which do you like best: chicken, beef, fish, or pork? Or are you a vegetarian?

Examples for adult students:

11. Do you have children?
12. Can you drive a car?
13. Would you rather watch TV, go to the movies, read a book, or go shopping?
14. If you could win one of the following, which would you prefer: a sports car? minivan? convertible? truck? sedan? sports utility vehicle?

Examples for multilingual students:

15. What country do you come from?
16. What language do you speak?

Procedure: Once students have interviewed each other and their assigned question has been answered, explain to them how they are to display the information on the board – simply in numbers or graphically using a bar or a pie chart.

Example using a bar chart:

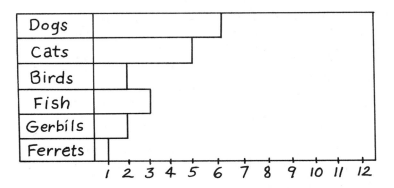

When the displays have been completed, use them as conversation starters. For example, if the display for question 1 reveals that some students have a dog, ask for a show of hands: "Who has a pet dog?" Ask each student, "What kind do you have? What is its name?" Similarly: "Who wants to visit Washington, D.C.? Who has already been there? What should Raven and Chih Mian see when they go there?"

Comment: If your class is large, this activity takes considerable time. You may want to devote one class period to the survey and a subsequent class to display and discussion.

B.2 Setting agendas

Although we usually have more goals and activities for our students to accomplish than we have time for, it is important, nevertheless, to include students in setting agendas whenever possible. Students often have their own agendas, which they usually share with us only when we ask them. In addition, students are likely to participate more wholeheartedly if they have a voice in determining what the goals and the means of achieving the goals are to be.

To that end, (1) try to involve students in setting daily, weekly, monthly, seasonal, or even longer-term agendas for the whole class, as well as for group and individual work. And, (2) whenever possible, give individual students, groups, or the whole class their choice of activities by:

- Writing a list of at least two or three choices on the board and having students select one (see Activity B.2.5, for example).
- Inviting students to add their own agenda items to a list but setting limits (for example, "Only one game" or "No field trips").
- Asking students to give you a list of, say, six possible suggestions for an agenda, from which they know you will select one or two.

Also, (3) stimulate your students to strive to achieve the goals you have set for them (see Activity B.2.2).

Finally, (4) use other activities in this section that are designed to help you involve your students in setting agendas and/or to show students how your agenda is based on their needs.

B.2.1 Personal pronunciation agendas
B.2.2 Keeping score
B.2.3 What's it all about? Prereading
B.2.4 What I learned from the reading assignment; what I want to know
B.2.5 Setting class, team, pair, or individual agendas
B.2.6 What we know about our community and what we need to find out: A project
B.2.7 Presenting a large-scale project

See also:

A.7.1 Targeting correct language use: Vocabulary, pronunciation, or grammar
A.7.4 What I learned from today's class; questions I have about today's material

B.2.1 Personal pronunciation agendas

Procedure: When you have been working on certain sounds that are difficult for your students to pronounce and you later hear a student mispronounce a word containing one of these sounds, write the word on the board along with the student's name or initials.

Tell students to look up the pronunciation in their notes or their dictionary or to ask for help. Encourage them to reuse the word during the class if they can, and tell them that they can erase their name or initials if they subsequently pronounce the word correctly.

Follow-up: Leave any remaining words on the board until the next class, if possible; or write them down, and, at the beginning of the next class, quickly check students' pronunciation of these words by pointing to them on the list.

Comment: Explain to students that the public posting of their errors will help them keep the problematic sound in their mind so that they can avoid repeating the error.

Try to post a number of students' names or initials on the board so as not to frustrate or embarrass an individual student, especially the first time you use this activity. If you continue to use the activity, students will soon realize that everyone has problems with certain sounds and that everyone's mistakes are posted sooner or later.

B.2.2 Keeping score

Encouraging, keeping track of, and rewarding language acquisition or academic performance.

Procedure: Choose one goal based on your students' needs. This goal might be attending class regularly, being on time, completing homework, participating in class discussions, raising hand to speak, working on pronunciation or grammar problems, using target vocabulary – whatever topic is important to you and your entire class or is currently being worked on.

Then draw a chart (such as the one on the next page) on a part of the board where it can remain undisturbed for the duration of this activity (or use a large sheet of newsprint), labeling the chart with the goal of the activity and listing each of your students' names along the left-hand margin of the chart. Be sure that you have enough space (enough grids) in which to note the number of times per class or the number of classes during which the goal is met.

Whenever a student successfully achieves the target goal, put an X (or an exclamation point) in the appropriate grid on the chart.

Content-based activities

Example:

Participating in discussion of today's homework

Anselmo	X	X	X								
Margarita	X	X	X	X							
Sebastian	X	X	X	X	X						
Sophia	X	X									

If the goal is such that students can earn checks frequently – such as correct use of a verb tense or class participation – you may want to keep a note of their successes on paper and enter the results at one time rather than as they occur in order to save yourself time and to avoid interrupting the class.

For some goals, students may enter their own achievement (e.g., attending class, arriving on time).

Variation: Start with the chart showing every student a winner and erase a segment when errors or lapses occur! This variation works especially well when the goal is pronouncing final -*s*!

Comments: You can choose different goals for different students or have your students set their own goals. You can use the same kind of chart for keeping team scores, too.

If your students like competition, you might want to offer a prize to the students who "wins." At the end of the class, the week, the term, or whatever time frame has been set, the student with the most X's next to his or her name might receive a prize appropriate to the goal and its duration, say, one jelly bean or a bag of jelly beans, a new pencil, or a dictionary. For competitive students, winning is often more important than the prize, but many do like the idea of receiving a prize.

B.2.3   What's it all about? Prereading

Preparation: Choose a reading from your course book or other source to assign as homework.

Procedure: In the class in which you assign the reading as homework, write the title of the reading on the board.

Then ask the students to think about the title and to predict, using only the title, what they think the reading will be about.

Write their predictions on the board next to the title.

Next, ask them to read the first paragraph of the reading; then ask them whether they want to revise their first predictions of what the reading will be about or to add any predictions. Write any revised or additional predictions near the original ones.

Explain to the class that these predictions are to serve as their agenda while they read the assignment and that they should note specific details in the reading that support a prediction as well as specific details that show that a prediction was incorrect.

Follow-up: Leave the predictions on the board until the next class, or copy them and rewrite them on the board before the next class.

At the next class, discuss with students why certain predictions about the meaning of the reading turned out to be correct but others did not.

Erase erroneous guesses, replacing them with correct information.

B.2.4   What I learned from the reading assignment; what I want to know

Preparation: During the class prior to this activity, assign as homework a reading from your course book or other source; or assign the reading as class work in preparation for the activity.

Procedure: Before discussing the assigned reading, ask as many students as can comfortably write on the board at the same time to write (1) one thing they learned from the reading assignment and (2) one question – either a question about something they didn't understand in the reading or something they would like to know more about.

You now have an agenda for class discussion of the reading assignment that is based on what some students already know and what they need to know or want to know.

Comment: A major benefit of this activity is that many students can "show what they know" publicly, whereas in a typical discussion of a reading, only a few students may get that opportunity.

Also, students may spontaneously begin the discussion by asking their peers about comments they have written on the board or by answering questions their peers have written there.

B.2.5 Setting class, team, pair, or individual agendas

Procedure: On the board write a list of assignments under the categories *writing, speaking and reading.* Have students consider which of these skills they most need to practice and then have them choose one assignment for their personal agenda. Have each student write her or his name next to the specific assignment she or he has chosen. If an assignment lends itself to group work, students who have chosen the same assignment will work together.

Because posting agendas publicly makes them more likely to be kept, keep each group's agenda on the board until the work is completed, or have students transfer their lists to paper and post them on a bulletin board.

Sample assignment list (students choose one):

Writing agenda:

- Write an article for a class newsletter.
- Create material for a class scrapbook (e.g., new drawings and writings or additions to selected prior assignments).
- Write a summary of a recent course book reading.

Speaking agenda:

- Prepare an oral presentation to teach your group or class how to do or make something.
- With a partner, prepare a mock debate of a current controversial issue to present to your group or whole class.
- Give an oral report of a movie or TV show you have seen recently.

Reading agenda:

- Read a short story or short essay: write a quiz about it to exchange with members of your group who have done the same assignment.
- Read something new in your course book. Make a list of each new word and then, using a dictionary, create a glossary for the reading to exchange with a classmate who has also done this task.
- Examine a current magazine. Decide who its audience is and write a review recommending (or not recommending) the magazine to your classmates, giving the reasons for your opinion. Exchange your review with your classmates who have also done this task and discuss any differences of opinion with them. If they have reviewed a different magazine, review their magazine while they review yours, and then discuss any differences of opinion with them.

Variation: For a larger block of time, require that students select one task from each agenda.

B.2.6 What we know about our community and what we need to find out: A project

For immigrant or international students (but see Variation 2 for EFL students).

Procedure: Ask your immigrant or international students to tell you what they already know about their new community, and record the information (or have a scribe record it) on the board. Ask them questions such as:

- What is the name of our main street? our local newspaper?
- At what channel (number) is our local TV station found? What are its call letters?
- At what channel (number) is our local radio station found? What are its call letters?
- In case of an emergency, what number do we dial to get help?
- Where is our post office? When is it open?
- Where is our bus station? train station? airport?
- Do we have a park? Where is it? What is its name?
- Do we have any public monuments? Where are they? Why were they built?
- Where is our public library? When is it open?
- What kind of local government do we have? Do we have a mayor? a town manager? What other local government officials are there? Where are their offices?
- Do we celebrate any special occasions or hold community events (e.g., a strawberry or harvest festival, public band concerts, parades, pancake breakfasts, fireworks)? If we do, when and where do they occur?

When you have gathered all the information from the students that you can, make a list on the board of questions they could not answer.

Follow-up: For homework, either assign one student to each unanswered question or allot the unanswered questions to small groups.

You may want to discuss where the information they need is likely to be found and rehearse polite ways to ask for information.

If you can, leave the unanswered questions on the board until the next class, when students assigned to the questions can write the answers next to the questions.

Variations:

1. Follow the same procedure using your state, province, county, or other geographical division instead of your local community.

    Ask for information such as:

    - Capital city
    - Head official's name and title

- Major cities, lakes, rivers
- Places of interest such as battlefields or monuments
- Types of industry and agriculture
- Mottoes

2. EFL students might do this activity using a geographical division located in an English-speaking country that they are studying or that particularly interests them, using people they know from the "target" community or, more likely, using the Internet to get the information.

B.2.7 Presenting a large-scale project

Procedure: For a large-scale project, use the board to help you and your students lay out goals, determine and assign jobs or other responsibilities, fix dates and deadlines, and plan follow-ups, if any.

Example: Creating an ESL newsletter

Discuss the newsletter with students and pick a target audience, such as other classes or levels in your school or perhaps the local community.

Then, using the board to record answers, brainstorm with the class:

1. The types of information that would interest the chosen audience
2. A name for your newsletter
3. The kinds of jobs involved in writing and publishing a newsletter such as:

- Editor
- Copy editor
- Entertainment reviewer
- Designer
- Distributor
- Feature writer
- Cartoonist or illustrator
- News reporter
- Publisher

Next, have students choose one or more jobs – or use a method such as drawing straws – and write the students' names next to their job(s).

Now, draw a mock-up of the newsletter on the board and have students decide where each article will go.

On the mock-up write the names of students who are responsible for each article.

Leave the mock-up on the board until the project is complete, or transfer the information to newsprint and tape the newsprint to a wall.

Finally, with students, determine a target date for completion of the newsletter, set deadlines for assignments, and arrange times to meet to review students' progress.

Write these dates and times on the board so that students can copy them into their notebooks.

Comment: Keep all information available for reference for the life of the project.

Variations: Other large-scale projects using this procedure could be:

- Going on a field trip
- Having a visitors' day
- Presenting a talent show
- Presenting a play
- Filming a video showing your school's various classes at work and at play

B.3 Sharing information, feelings, and opinions

Activities B.3.1 through B.3.3 empower students by having them assume the teacher's role of gathering information and presenting it in the classroom. Activities B.3.4 through B.3.6 enable students to air their feelings and opinions.

B.3.1 Scavenging for signs
B.3.2 Scavenging for answers
B.3.3 Mapping information
B.3.4 A message in a bottle
B.3.5 How does it rank?
B.3.6 How does it rate?

See also:

B.2.5 Setting class, team, pair, or individual agendas (see Speaking and Reading agendas for information-sharing and opinion-sharing activities)
B.2.6 What we know about our community and what we need to find out: A project (an information-sharing activity)

B.3.1 Scavenging for signs

Procedure: To encourage your immigrant or international students to read the signs that surround them every day, assign a scavenger hunt for signs. For homework, ask them, for example, to find signs that contain the following:

- A mention of food
- The word *sale*
- A mention of an occupation
- A price
- A command
- A period of time, e.g., day(s) of the week or hours
- Only one word

- A person's name
- The word *no*
- An abbreviation
- A warning
- Something funny
- An illustration

Students should find one or more signs for as many categories as possible. Once students find a sign that fits a category, they should record it in their notebook or journal, along with its physical description (shape, colors) and location (e.g., on a bus or in a restaurant window).

When the students have completed the assignment, look over their results.

Select one or more students to draw on the board an example for each category and to tell the class where their sign is located, what it looks like (size, shape, colors), and why (or whether) they think the sign is needed.

Students who like to draw will probably want their drawing to display the size and shape of their sign and to use appropriately colored chalk or markers.

Comment: You may want to preface this assignment by modeling the activity, drawing one or two signs you've seen and explaining what they mean.

B.3.2 Scavenging for answers

Interviewing English speakers and presenting information to peers.

Procedure: To encourage students to (1) speak with English speakers outside of the classroom, (2) seek out information on their own that is difficult to find in a book, and (3) present that information to their peers, send them on a scavenger hunt to ask English speakers about idioms.

First, prepare a list of idioms and assign one or more to each student. You may want to choose a theme, such as idioms that use a part of the body (e.g., *elbow grease* or *as plain as the nose on your face*). However, if your students have limited access to speakers of English outside of the classroom – particularly to native speakers – you may not want to restrict the assignment to certain types of idioms but just ask students to gather idioms in general.

When you receive the students' work, look over the results. Select the best of each student's answers for the student to write on the board and to explain to the class.

Having the material written on the board eliminates misunderstandings by other students that might be caused by pronunciation problems. Also, the other members of the class can copy the information into their notebooks for review and future reference. Further, board writing helps fix the information in the presenter's memory.

Comment: Students may need to practice their interviewing skills on their peers – that is, explaining the purpose for their questions, asking for information, and verifying their comprehension – before they approach their potential respondents outside of the classroom.

Variations: Follow the same procedure using slang words or words with certain suffixes (such as *-ous* or *-ity*) or homonyms (*die/dye*) – but students should be aware that many native speakers may need to be told what a *homonym* is and to be given an example before they can provide other examples.

Again, students can ask their respondents for examples in general, or you can give students lists and ask them to find out what the listed items mean.

If you use lists for homonyms, you can give students the half of the pair that is more common and ask them to find out how the mates are spelled and what they mean, for example,

rain/_____
poor/_____
air/_____

Another fun and useful topic to use is gestures (respondents should probably be native speakers). Have students query their respondents to find out what gestures are used to express certain concepts. Of course, this topic requires students to demonstrate their findings for their peers rather than use the board to illustrate.

Some gestures students might be asked to find out about are the following:

Be quiet	OK
I don't know	I can't hear you
Come here	Good-bye

Good idea, good job, I like it	Bad idea, bad job, I don't like it
Use the telephone	That person is crazy
I smell something bad	It's expensive (money)
Hurry up	A very little amount (tiny)
I'm puzzled	Sit down next to me
I'm thinking	It was hard work
Wait a moment	

Acknowledgment: This activity first appeared in a different format in Jeannine Dobbs, "Scavenge for Answers," in Nikhat Shameem and Makhan Tickoo (eds.), *New Ways in Using Communicative Games in Language Teaching* (1999).

B.3.3 Mapping information

Sharing information about a country of interest while practicing grammatical constructions.

Procedure for monolingual EFL classes: On the board draw a large map of the country in which you are teaching and a map of a predominantly English-speaking country which your class is studying or in which you and they are interested.

Brainstorm with students what is known about the two countries.

Then indicate graphically – colored chalk or markers can be used – and label items such as terrain, climate, areas of dense or sparse population, and areas where specific crops are grown, minerals are mined, and animals are raised.

Use the maps to provide students with practice of grammatical constructions such as:

- Comparisons: X is larger than Y.
- Passive voice: Wheat is grown in . . .
- There is . . ./there are . . . constructions: There is a lot of wheat in . . .; there are many mountains in . . . .

Follow-up: If the initial brainstorming for information regarding the English-speaking country elicits little response, assign as homework the gathering of additional information from atlases and encyclopedias (preferably written in English), from the Internet, or from interviews with people outside the classroom who are familiar with the chosen country.

Variation for multilingual classes: On the board draw a large map of the country in which you are teaching. Have students, working in groups

Content-based activities

Example:

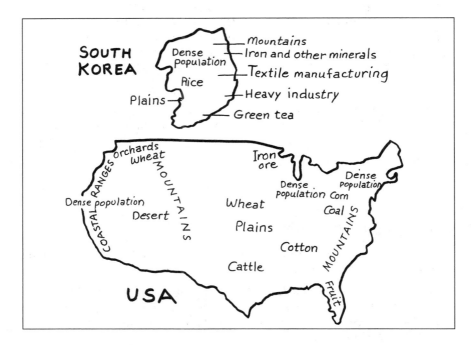

based on their nationality or the region where they are from, draw their countries or regions.

Proceed as above.

Comment: If you have a very large class and/or limited board space, have some groups work at their seats drawing and marking maps of their countries.

As time permits, have these students replace their peers' maps with their own and verbally describe their maps using the desired grammatical constructions.

Acknowledgment: This activity is based on one in Peter Shaw and Theresa deVet, *Using Blackboard Drawing* (1980).

B.3.4 A message in a bottle

Procedure: Explain that the purpose of this activity is to write messages that could be placed in a bottle to be cast into the ocean and would introduce the class to the finder. On the board, draw a very large bottle with enough room for several students to write messages inside of it (or, if your class is large, draw several bottles).

Divide the class into groups. Each group is to use its brainstorming and negotiating skills to decide on its message. Limit the number of words to, say, thirty.

When the groups have decided on their messages, have a scribe from each group write her or his group's message inside the bottle(s) you have drawn. Allow time for each group to compare what the others wrote and to discuss what each thought was important to say.

Variations:

1. Instead of putting a message in a bottle, have students compose a message to be placed aboard a space shuttle bound for another planet to explain our civilization to alien life forms or to future space travelers. In this case, draw a large space shuttle on the board for their messages.
2. Have students write a message describing life on earth today, to be placed in a time capsule that will be opened in the year 2100. Draw a large time capsule to contain the board writing.

B.3.5   How does it rank?

Group rankings based on discussing, reasoning, and comparing.

Procedure:

1. Write a topic on the board such as the following.

   • The best pet
   • The most important ingredients for a successful party

- The qualities of a successful language learner
- The qualities of a good teacher
- Things that would make the world a better place in which to live

2. Ask students to brainstorm the topic and list as many answers as they can.
3. Write or have a scribe write their contributions on the board.
4. Ask each student to rank the items on the list, putting the most important item at the top and the least important at the bottom.
5. Now divide the class into three to five small groups, each with a discussion leader, a reporter to take notes during the discussion and later to do board writing, and a timekeeper. Have each group discuss each member's individual listing and then compose a group list. You will need to set a time limit of, say, ten minutes, on this part of the task because some students take much longer than others to do it. Tell groups that finish first to think of additional items and insert them in their list.
6. When the group listings are complete, have group reporters write their group's list on the board and present the reasons why the group chose the order the items are in.
7. Have the whole class discuss the lists, and if time allows and interest remains, create a class ranking.

   One way to cut the time required for this last step is to alter the task from ranking to classifying. Have students group their responses as follows: Crucial, Very important, Important, and Not so important. This allows them to continue using comparisons but doesn't require their making fine distinctions.

B.3.6 How does it rate?

Forming, supporting, and debating opinions.

Preparation: Select a controversial statement, perhaps drawn from your course book or other reading that you plan to work on during the next class.

Procedure: Write the material you have selected on the board, and under it draw a table on which to enter your students' opinions.

Do not allow discussion at this time; ask students to tell you where to place their initials.

Example:
When in Rome, do as the Romans do.

Strongly Disagree									Strongly Agree
1	2	3	4	5	6	7	8	9	10
MT	E	P		J	D	MD	TF		
TH	H	N	A			O		K	
F	B	U					MC		

Once you have completed the table but before any discussion begins, you might want to instruct students to brainstorm – either individually or with those who hold basically the same opinion as they do – to determine some reasons why they feel the way they do. This permits them to more fully explore their feelings before hearing opposing views that might too easily dissuade them from supporting their initial reactions.

Next, do one of the following.

- Use the results of your graphic survey of students' opinions to help you orchestrate a lively whole-class discussion.
- Place students into pro and con groups for a debate.
- Place students into smaller discussion groups in which both sides of the issue are represented.
- Place students into other groupings as suggested by the results; for example, do the responses reflect any similarities based on gender or, if your class is international, on nationality?

Content-based activities

Comment: If you have students who can't decide because they believe that their opinion would depend on the specific situation, ask them to answer "in principle" or "for the sake of argument."

Additional examples of controversial statements:

- It's better to have loved and lost than never to have loved at all.
- Incurably ill patients should be allowed to die if they want to.
- There's little or nothing an individual can do about the problem of global warming.

Variation: Rate opinions (agree or disagree) on characters, situations, or deeds from the assigned course book or other reading, such as:

- In Damon Runyan's short story "Butch Minds the Baby," Big Butch is a sympathetic character.
- The crew that took to the lifeboats during the *Titanic* disaster are more to be pitied than condemned for leaving people to drown in order to save their own lives, since they had to live the rest of their lives with that deed on their conscience.
- The mayor did the right thing in forbidding the carnival to set up in our town when it was learned that one of the rides had safety problems.

Students from the author's ESL class at Southern New Hampshire University celebrating the end of the summer term (1994).

Appendix A
Electronic whiteboards

The ultimate board, the electronic whiteboard, has great potential as a teaching tool and may someday make chalkboards and regular whiteboards obsolete, especially in affluent schools.

Electronic whiteboards already offer some amazing features. Some are small enough to be portable; others are large enough to cover a wall. Some are interactive, so that not only the teacher but also the students may take control of what appears there. Information to be displayed to a class may be typed on a keyboard or may be written directly on the whiteboard. Either way, the information can then be saved to the hard drive of a computer, where it can be edited or immediately printed for distribution in black and white or, in the case of some types of whiteboard, printed in whatever colors were used in the original writing. In some cases, the images may also be faxed or sent as e-mail attachments. In addition, when not in use electronically, some computerized whiteboards can be used as a regular dry-erase white-board.

Electronic whiteboards have application not only as classroom tools but also as tools to facilitate distance learning. All it will take is money to make available a process (described by Stephen Giles of the Computer Technology Department at Monash University, Melbourne, Australia) employing a terminal-mounted camera with sound facilities, together with an electronic whiteboard plus PowerPoint or other graphics programs, to produce a packaged lecture capable of being accessed by students at a distance in very close to real time.

All things considered, electronic whiteboards would seem to be the board of the future for those able to afford them.

Appendix B
Providing alternative public writing surfaces

Turning your wall into a chalkboard

It is possible to turn an ordinary wall into a black or green chalkboard surface using a commercial slating product available at many hardware, paint, or discount stores. To purchase all the ingredients you will need to make up to 50 square feet of chalkboard writing surface should cost less than $50 in the United States. Because the slating product needs time to dry between coats and to cure, about 60 hours will be needed from beginning to end to create your new board.

You can also restore old chalkboard surfaces using a coat of the slating product.

A whiteboard alternative

A small-scale version of a whiteboard-like writing surface is available in "cling" sheets that can be attached to a wooden or plaster wall or to a window by mere static electricity. The sheets can be written on with whiteboard markers, erased and reused, taken down and put back up, and rolled up and carried to other rooms or other schools. They come in several dimensions, from notebook to newsprint size. In the United States they can be purchased from many office supply stores for, currently, about $20 per tablet of twenty newsprint-sized sheets.

Some drawbacks include the fact that if they are rolled too soon after the writing is done, they smear; if they are not erased promptly, they do not erase thoroughly. But the advantage of having an extra, easily portable, flexible board space – or, for some teachers, access to public writing where none was possible before – would seem to outweigh these inconveniences.

References

Bibliography

Brookes, Mona, *Drawing with Children: A Creative Method for Adult Beginners, Too,* Putnam, New York, 1996.

Clark, Ray, "Second Thoughts on Vocabulary," Northern New England TESOL Spring Conference, 1994.

Dauer, Rebecca M., *Accurate English: A Complete Course in Pronunciation,* Prentice Hall Regents, Paramus, N.J., 1993.

Dobbs, Jeannine. "Scavenge for Answers," in Nikhat Shameem and Makhan Tickoo (eds.), *New Ways in Using Communicative Games in Language Teaching,* TESOL, Alexandria, Va., 1999.

Doff, Adrian, *Teach English: A Training Course for Teachers,* Cambridge University Press, Cambridge, 1988.

Edwards, Betty, *Drawing on the Artist Within,* Simon and Schuster, New York, 1986.

Edwards, Betty, *Drawing on the Right Side of the Brain,* Collins, New York, 1993.

Fagin, Larry, *The List Poem: A Guide to Teaching & Writing Catalog Verse,* Teachers and Writers Collaborative, New York, 1991.

Gibaldi, Joseph, *MLA Handbook for Writers of Research Papers,* 4th ed., The Modern Language Association of America, New York, 1995.

Giegerich, Heinz, J., *English Phonology: An Introduction,* Cambridge University Press, Cambridge, 1992.

Giles, Stephen, "An Electronic Whiteboard in the Lecture Theatre," <www.monash.edu.au/hepcit/010896p.htm> (May 26, 1998).

Grant, Linda, *Well Said: Advanced English Pronunciation,* Heinle & Heinle, Boston, 1993.

Hagen, Stacy A., and Patricia E. Grogan, *Sound Advantage: A Pronunciation Book,* Prentice Hall Regents, Paramus, N.J., 1992.

Hutchinson, Helene D., *ESL Teacher's Book of Instant Word Games for Grades 7–12,* Prentice Hall, Paramus, N.J., 1997.

Kirn, Elaine, *Scenario 1: English Grammar in Context,* Holt, Rinehart and Winston, Austin, Tex., 1984.

Lalonda, Lori, "Dave's ESL Cafe: Dave's ESL Idea Page," <www.eslcafe.com> (July 1997).

Lane, Linda, *Focus on Pronunciation: Principles and Practice for Effective Communication,* Longman, White Plains, N.Y., 1993.

Lee, W. R., *Language Teaching Games and Contests,* Oxford University Press, Oxford, 1987.

Levy, Tedd, "First in His Class: The Many Contributions of Samuel Read Hall," *Magazine of History,* Vol. 6, No. 2, Fall, 1991, pp. 38–41.

References

MLA Handbook . . . , *see under* Gibaldi.

Murphy, Chris, "Dave's ESL Cafe: ESL Ideas from 1996," <www.eslcafe.com> (June 15, 1998).

O'Hare, Michael, "Talk and Chalk: The Blackboard as an Intellectual Tool,"*Journal of Policy Analysis & Management,* Vol. 12, No. 1, Winter, 1993, pp. 239–246.

Pollard, Laurel, and Natalie Hess, *Zero Prep: Ready to Go Activities for the Language Classroom,* Alta, Burlingame, Calif., 1997.

Rinvolucri, Mario, *Grammar Games: Cognitive, Affective and Drama Activities for ESL Students,* Cambridge University Press, Cambridge, 1984.

Robinson, Adam, and the Staff of *The Princeton Review, Word Smart: Building an Educated Vocabulary,* Villard, New York, 1994.

Shapiro, Norma, and Carol Genser, *Chalk Talks,* Command Performance Language Institute, Berkeley, 1994.

Shaw, Peter, and Therese deVet, *Using Blackboard Drawing,* Heinemann, Portsmouth, N.H., 1980.

Spenser, Dwight, *Word Games in English,* Regents, New York, N.Y., 1976.

Ur, Penny, *Grammar Practice Activities: A Practical Guide for Teachers,* Cambridge University Press, Cambridge, 1988.

Woonton, Nanette, "Dave's ESL Cafe: Dave's ESL Idea Page," <www.eslcafe.com> (June 15, 1998).

Wright, Andrew, *Pictures for Language Learning,* Cambridge University Press, Cambridge, 1990.

Wright, Andrew, and Safia Haleem, *Visuals for the Language Classroom,* Longman, White Plains, N.Y., 1991.

Yates, John, "Using the Blackboard," *TESL Talk,* Vol. 12, No. 3, Summer, 1981, 48–61.

Yorkey, Richard, *Checklists for Vocabulary Study,* Addison-Wesley, Reading, Mass., 1981.

Further reading

Bassano, Sharon, and Mary Ann Christison, *Drawing Out: Second Language Acquisition through Student-Created Images,* Alemany Press, Paramus, N.J., 1982.

Dobbs, Jeannine, "The Blackboard as an Active/Interactive Language Teaching Tool," *College ESL,* Vol. 7, No. 2, December, 1997.

Mugglestone, Patricia, *Planning and Using the Blackboard,* Heinemann, Portsmouth, N.H., 1980.

Rasmussen, Greta, *The Great Unbored Blackboard Book,* Tin Man Press, Stanwood, Wash., 1985.

Index

Names of activities are in bold type.

Index